ABOUT THE
AMERICA'S
CUP

ABOUT THE
AMERICA'S
CUP

By
Vernon Hines

In Collaboration With
Writer: James T. Bernath

Bookcliff Publishing Company
Grand Junction, Colorado
USA

i

Library of Congress
Catalogue Card No. 86-072354

ISBN: 0-940089-00-9

Bookcliff Publishing Company
Grand Junction, Colo. 81502

Produced in the United States of America
First printing, October 1986

TO MY WONDERFUL WIFE

WINNIE

Acknowledgments

The author would like to thank:
Geneva Curry, Peter Newman, manager America's Cup Information Center, Red and Jean Paulin, Louis Vuitton Cup Information Center, Royal Perth Yacht Club. The Syndicates: America's Cup 1987 Defence Ltd.; America II Challenge; BNZ America's Cup Challenge; British America's Cup Challenge; Challenge KIS France; Consorzio Azzurra Sfide Italiana America's Cup; Consorzio Italia; Courageous Challenge; Canada's Challenge for the America's Cup; Eagle Challenge; Eastern Australian America's Cup Defence; Golden Gate Challenge; Heart of America Challenge; Sail America; Southern Australian Challenge for the Defence of the 1987 America's Cup; Taskforce 1987 Defence.

Illustrations by Phyllis McClellan

About the Author

The author, Vernon Hines, was born in 1917 at Newkirk, Okla. As a boy and young man he worked on ranches in Oklahoma and Texas and in Texas oil fields. He attended school eight years in a number of places, including Oklahoma City, Arkansas City, Kan., and Sugarland and Dallas, Texas. He attended one year at the University of Houston.

Hines enlisted in the Army during World War II. He attended the field artillery officer candidate's school at Fort Sill, Okla., and later became a field artillery captain and battery commander. He served in the Aleutian Islands and in Europe, receiving the silver and bronze stars, the commendation medal and the presidential unit citation.

Hines embarked on a career in manufacturing in the combustion engineering field in 1946. In 1948 he moved to Denver where he owned and operated a manufacturing and engineering company until 1982. He holds patents in the automotive, heating, air conditioning and process piping fields. His professional memberships include the American Institute Aeronautics and Astronautics, American Society of Refrigeration and Air Conditioning Engineers, the National Association of Power Engineers and Colorado Society of Engineers.

A long-time boating enthusiast and golfer, Hines is the former owner of the Peck House in Empire, Colo., the oldest operating hotel-restaurant in the state.

Hines, an active member of the El Jebel Shrine, for many years raised harness horses for racing and is a collector of native American art. He owns Red Men Hall in Empire, which is one of the finest American Indian art galleries in the Rockies.

CONTENTS

Illustrations

Photos of 12-Meter Yachts

Charts and Maps

The Cup in Brief

The America's Cup is 27 inches tall and has 134 ounces of silver wrought by Garrard's of London in 1848 at the request of the Royal Yacht Squadron of Cowes, England.

Originally known as the 100 Guineas Cup, it was offered to the winner of a fleet race held Aug. 22, 1851. The Royal Yacht Squadron sponsored the regatta in which some of the swiftest sailboats of the day raced 53 miles around the Isle of Wight off Cowes.

It was just the sort of thing for boat builder and future commodore of the New York Yacht Club John Stevens, who had provided the impetus for building a boat that would not only win a tidy wager for him but one that would prove that American sailing and design skills were second to none.

The boat Stevens and other New York businessmen commissioned for the race was the *America*. It won the 100 Guineas Cup in the regatta, which had been open to all nations. The trophy was brought to the United States and would not leave its eastern shore again for another 132 years. In 1857 Stevens donated it to the New York Yacht Club under the proviso that it always remain a perpetual trophy to be competed for on a friendly basis by all interested nations meeting the basic qualifications.

The first challenge for the Cup didn't surface until 1870, but except for the stormy years of World War I and II the contest generally has been held every several years since. The America's Cup series of 1958 was contested with a new type of racer, the 12-meter yacht. Since that series interest has steadily increased in what is now a truly international sporting event and a multi-million-dollar affair for those who would seek the Cup.

Glossary of Terms for Sailing and the America's Cup

Abaft — to the rear of, towards the stern

Abeam — on a line at right angles to a ship's keel

Aft — toward or at the rear or stern of a ship

America's Cup — a silver, Victorian-era trophy offered since 1857 on a perpetual basis to nations competing in the sailing race by the same name

Astern — at the rear of or behind a ship

Ballast — the heavy weight, particularly lead, placed in a keel to give a ship stability

Bearing — direction a ship is headed

Boom — spar at the foot of a sail

Bow — forward part of a ship

Beat, Beating — zig-zag or tacking motion of a boat attempting to sail into the wind

Bitter end — the extreme tail end of the anchor cable, rope or chain; if you see it could be bitter

Centerboard — retractable keel used in sailboats

Clew — metal loop connected to the lower corner of a sail

Challenger — the racing syndicate representing a yacht club and which is entered in an America's Cup series in order to compete for the silver cup

Challenger trials — series of elimination races among racing syndicates representing yacht clubs from competing nations to determine which will race in the finals against the defending syndicate and yacht club

Clipper — fast sailing ship with tall, raking masts, a large sail area and long, slender lines

Close-hauled — having the sails set for sailing as nearly against the wind as a ship will go

Cover — when a ship sails in front of and directly between

a pursuing ship and the direction of the wind

Cutter — fore- and aft-rigged sailing vessel with a jib, forestaysail, mainsail and single mast

Defender — the yacht club which holds the America's Cup and therefore must organize a defense campaign and select a syndicate to defend the trophy; also the syndicate representing that yacht club

Defense trials — series of elimination races among syndicates representing yacht clubs within a country holding the Cup to determine which will race against a challenger

Dinghy — a small rowboat or sailboat

Downhill, downwind — in the direction the wind is blowing

Draft, draught — the depth of water a ship draws

Freeboard — distance between the waterline and deck

Grinder — large winch for hoisting or trimming a sail

Guy — rope that steadies or supports a spar

Halyard — rope or wire for hoisting and lowering a sail

Helm — steering wheel of a ship

Hull — main body of a boat

Genoa — large sail foreward of the mast

Jib — triangular sail set foreward of the mast

Jibe or gybe — to change a ship's course by switching the sails from one side to the other when the wind is behind and thereby bringing the stern across the wind

Keel — type of fin extending below a boat, which provides balance and stability

Lay day — a day off from racing called for by competitors for the America's Cup or in other sailing contests

Leeward — situated away from the wind or downwind

Luff — act of suddenly heading into or sailing a ship closer to the wind

Mainsail — principal sail on the main mast

Mainsheet — rope used to secure and trim the mainsail

Mark — any one of the bouys on an America's Cup course

marking the end of a leg and beginning of another

Match race — race between only two ships

Port — left side of a ship

Reach — when the wind is blowing from the side of a ship

Rig — the shape, number and arrangement of sails and masts on a ship

Schooner — fore- and aft-rigged sailing ship with three to seven masts

Sheet — rope used to trim a sail

Sloop — fore- and aft-rigged sailing ship with one mast and a single headsail jib

Spinnaker — large triangular and parachutelike sail used when running before or with the wind.

Starboard — right side of a ship

Stern — rear part or area of a ship

Syndicate — common name for the organization that finances a race on behalf of a yacht club

Tack, tacking — when a ship follows a zig-zag course either to remain ahead of or overtake another ship or what a ship does when it beats against the wind

Tender — the boat that carries supplies, various equipment and staff, and which accompanies a racing boat out to the course

Time on distance — at the start of a sailing race, a calculation of the time it will take to cover the distance from where a boat is to the starting line either at the same time or just after the starting gun is fired

To leeward — in the direction the wind is blowing

To weather — into the wind

Transom — a crosspiece at the stern of a ship

Trim — to adjust a sail in order to get maximum wind power

Trim tab — a rudder attached to the keel of a boat

Windward — into the wind

Introduction

Having friends in Australia and an idea in mind was all it took to prompt my wife, Winnie, and me to take a trip Down Under in March 1986.

What a country — but first the idea.

Through the years the America's Cup struck me as a gentleman's race for the wealthy who donned blue blazers, white pants and slick dogs that could grip the deck of a yacht; this was a diversion intended only for the Harold Vanderbilts and Sir Thomas Liptons of this world. After some checking in early 1986, however, such myths faded as it became apparent the Cup was far more than a rich man's pastime.

The America's Cup was in fact as bona fide a sporting contest as any, waged with a ferocity like no other and rich in tradition and style. Million-dollar yachts, yes, and backed by those of means, but these jewels of the ocean scraped and rammed one another, battled like sloops and cutters of old, and the warriors in the fray were as talented and well trained as any sportsmen. These sailors were tough and dedicated, took leave from their professions for years at a time and for virtually no reward, save the chance to participate in what people characterize as sailing's greatest race.

Yes, the wealthy continue to be the driving force for a contest that is naturally costly, but they are sports, too, and some are worth admiring — men like Alan Bond, who apparently had everything in the world one could want — but he didn't have the silver cup. So he set out after it with the same tenacity he'd employed in building a financial empire, and spent nearly a decade and tens of millions of dollars to acquire it. Then there was the gracious tea mogul, Sir Thomas Lipton, who spent 30 years on the same quest and never fulfilled his dream. Yet, here was the classic sportsman, a man who as much as anyone and

1

anything throughout its history had made the America's Cup the great contest that it is.

Why? I wanted to know more, to know when, where, why and how it all began, but where was it recorded? Except for news accounts there just wasn't much around and there was so much to know about the Cup's 135-year history. Where were the basic facts that could bring the curious up to the present and provide the basis for intelligently viewing future Cup matches? Especially the 1987 America's Cup at Fremantle, Australia. It had been billed around the world as the international sporting event of the year and certainly the most publicized and anticipated series ever. And how did it get to Australia? America ruled the waves, didn't it?

Upon additional checking, I discovered the information was out there, but in bits and pieces. There were so many different sources. The average person who wanted to know more wouldn't have the resources or the time to track down all the salient facts. At least not in time for the October trials in which 17 yacht-racing syndicates would begin competing for three grueling months to determine which would defend the Cup for Australia and who in the rest of the world would try to take it away.

It would be great to read what sailors and others had to say about how the Cup was won or lost, who was the biggest rammer of them all and who spied on whom to gain the edge in design, but I wanted to know the basics about the Cup and before, not after the races. What about all of those beautiful 12-meter yachts? I wanted to know about them before they packed up their sails and returned to their home ports. I wanted to know more about these computer-based boats that are born of thousands of hours of the most sophisticated technology on the planet and fashioned of space-age materials.

Introduction

Of course, the sailing industry and sailing enthusiasts around the world will reap benefits from it all, too. With sailing being one of the fastest growing forms of recreation among the general public in the United States and many other countries — it's practically a national pastime in Australia — the America's Cup was producing better and better designs and materials and serving to increase accessibility for more and more people.

Now, wouldn't it be nice, I mused, if there were a book that included the following: an indication of how sailing got started and developed over time; some history of the Cup; how Australia got the Cup away from the New York Yacht Club; some basic information about the boats and what has to be done on them during a race; what the World 12-Meter Fleet Racing Championships in early 1986 portended for the 1987 Cup match; all the pertinent information on the 1987 contest — the boats, the syndicates and the sailors; and since Australia had the Cup and it is such a fascinating country, a little something about the land Down Under. Best of all, what if this book were to come out during the trials, be available for the series from start to finish and be broad enough to be useable long afterward.

ABOUT THE AMERICA'S CUP is such a book, but before I decided positively to undertake the project, we took that trip to Australia, the nation that brought tears to the eyes of the members of the New York Yacht Club in 1983.

We left Grand Junction, Colo., March 4, flew to Los Angeles, then on to Honululu all in less than six hours. Another 10 hours and we touched down in Sydney, one of the most beautiful cities in the world.

It was lunch at Bailey's in King's Cross — wonderful salads — then a ride on the Manley Ferry to the picturesque oceanside suburb by the same name. Dinner at K's Snapper Inn on the beach was a treat, and while you're dining on fresh seafood, if you look away from the bright lights of the city towards the South Pacific Ocean, you'll see the constellation, Southern Cross.

March 7, after a full day of sightseeing with friends Glynn and Sugar Jones in Old Sydney, Manley, Woolloomooloo and the fabulous Sydney Opera House, we had dinner and danced at the Royal Motor Yacht Club. As vice-commodore of the Western El Jebel Mariner's Club at Lake Powell in southeastern Utah, I was treated with such warmth and friendliness I felt like one of their own, albeit from 12,000 miles away.

We hated to leave Sydney, and just had to return to Old Sydney one last time. Still remember the Cowboy From Down Under, a quaint little shop that sells a wealth of American Indian jewelry and art work.

Four hours and 20 minutes aboard Ansett Airlines flight 240 and we were in Perth, the City of Light. This is a wonderful city. There to meet us were Red and Jean Paulin, who showed us such a marvelous time during our stay.

You can never see everything in a new place, but Kings Park, overlooking the Swan River — named long ago for the enchanting black swans in the area — is a gorgeous place from which to take in the entire spread of Perth.

The next day we were off to Yanchep National Park, 40 minutes north of Perth, where we witnessed those things that make Australia so curious to the rest of the world: koalas that didn't mind being fed by people; kookaburras all around; a mother kangaroo with a baby in her pouch — a delightful sight; and we still can recall the strange feeling of watching at least a hundred of those untamable black parrots stream past us.

Introduction

We visited Alan Bond's Sun City, similar to the one in Arizona, and then we visited Alan Bond's trophy, the America's Cup. Well, actually it belongs to the Royal Perth Yacht Club, but Bond and company put it there in 1983. Seeing the prize, I knew I wanted to know more about it all and that others would, too.

Down the Swan 11 miles is Fremantle where we visited the Fremantle Sailing Club, walked the marina and saw the handsome tender for the French Kiss, one of the many 12-meter yachts entered in the 1987 America's Cup, this one by the Challenge KIS syndicate out of Sete, France.

Red and I paid a visit to Peter Newman, manager of the America's Cup information Center. He provided me with a lot of valuable information and augmented my enthusiasm when he said the idea for the book seemed to be just the ticket at just the right time.

Now the Cup was on my mind all the time, but I have to at least mention Papa Luigis restaurant, which happens to be one of Fremantle's big attractions, not because there isn't much else in this bustling port town that was soon to be inundated with tens of thousands of sailing fans — because there's a great deal to see and do in Fremantle and Perth — but because this Italian eatery is terrific.

While the idea for About the America's Cup seemed more inviting all the time, the whole idea of Australia was equally so during our four-week stay. Everywhere we went the people were as warm and friendly as could be.

In addtition to its people and beauty, Australia made us especially happy for several reasons: me, because there was some of the best fishing in the world; Winnie, because from Sydney to Fremantle the shopping was plentiful and pleasant;

and both of us because you can golf just about everywhere you go — the Aussies are great and avid golfers.

We even golfed on Rottnest Island about 13 miles off the coast of Fremantle. This is the small mass of land which helps to produce the fabled Fremantle Doctor, the wicked wind that plays havoc with boats that dare to sail off Western Australia's coast. Rottnest is a secret worth guarding, with its rare, little marsupial quokkas that looked like rats to the Dutch, who then named the place "rat nest," and its bowling greens and lovely lakes. Hundreds of thousands of visitors were planned for in the state of Western Australia, due largely to the Cup. So the island was sure to be discovered like so much else of this largest and most geographically contrasting of the country's states with its Mediterraneanlike, desolate-desert interior and the remote frontier of the north. Some of the world's finest sailors were converging on this marvelous place for the biggest races of their lives but they were to be equally envied for having the opportunity to see this beautiful land.

Just a few brief comments about the book:

ABOUT THE AMERICA'S CUP tries to do one thing above all else — present the interesting and pertinent information surrounding the America's Cup in such a manner that the sailor, sailing enthusiast and even the unenthused, but curious, can pick it up and learn some things about the contest and its development. The contents of these pages were selected and interpreted from a wide range of background materials.

The quantity of information for each of the racing syndicates in chapter VI was not entirely determined on the basis of its potential success in the 1987 America's Cup or on past success, rather it was partly dependent on the information that was available, including that which was provided by the syndicates themselves; some provided a wealth of information, others provided very little.

The book is informational in nature and not given to forecasts or personal preferences. Thus, there was neither a personal attempt to decide which are the better syndicates and what their chances are, though experts and general opinion are cited on those points, nor was there the intentional inclusion of any value judgments regarding the rightness or wrongness of anything said or done by individuals or groups in the present or past.

Finally, as an American, with more than a bit of nationalistic pride and competitive spirit prompts me to state for the record that I'm always for the Yanks — any of them — bringing the Cup back to America, but Australia seems to have given it a very comfortable resting place. I'm sure the Auld Mug would be equally well looked after and revered by any of the other 1987 hopefuls — Canada, Britain, France, Italy and New Zealand — or the scores of other seafaring nations, all of whom have perpetual invitations to pursue it.

Vernon Hines

Chapter I

Sailing Through Time

Man sailed in and perfected a thousand different boats over many thousands of years before the coming of the America's Cup, the world's most well-known sailboat race.

The design and construction expertise that go into today's boats were gleaned over the millenia by thousands of people through the process of trial and error.

The earliest boats were not pointed like those of the present, rather they were round like the coracle of the ancient Britons. These peculiar, basketlike vessels were nearly as broad as they were long and like all ancient craft were relatively small compared to the enormous ocean liners of today.

From antiquity to the present the sailing ship has journeyed from being a small craft not much larger than a dinghy, to the majestic, multi-masted warships and traders of the 17th and 18th centuries, to the great passenger vessels of the 19th century, and then quickly back to the smaller and sleeker, but more efficient craft of the 20th century.

Myriad shapes and sizes of sails and hulls have been tried and they've been fabricated of countless materials. Sailing ships with one mast and 10 masts, one hull and two hulls, one rudder and two rudders have at one time or another sailed the ocean blue.

The cargoes of sailing ships have been man's goods of necessity and those of luxury, of good sailors and bad sailors, slaves and freemen, convicts and their jailers, settlers and refugees, soldiers and ambassadors, toilers and travelers.

Young urban sailors have fashioned sailboats of rubber bands, Popcicle sticks and paper, and have managed grand gutter runs the length of entire city blocks. Others have taken slightly larger craft out for outings around the bay. Still others have sailed on glorious adventures around the world.

Throughout most of civilization sailing ships, both crude and sophisticated, have been used to further the economic interests of peoples around the world, but for much of that time they have also been used by many for diversion, including racing. It is hard to imagine the sailors and spectators of antiquity being any less enthusiastic over a well-contested race than modern-day yachtsmen and fans.

Racing on the Ar

It's late of an August afternoon, and long shadows line the east bank of the mighty Ar River.

Nearby, villages stand deserted, but here, along the Ar, where there is but an occasional gathering of so many, there is great laughter, singing, brief encounters between hurried voices and much scurrying about to find the best vantage point from which to view an impending event.

The fading sun barely glistens on the brown bodies of eager spectators who have come from villages near and far for this event — the traditional boat race to determine who will be chief boatman on the annual trading expedition.

Through a long and arduous process of elimination that includes not only measuring a man's seagoing skills, but many other factors as well, this year's competition has matched two of the finest boatmen the region has ever produced. In this desert place where the Ar is life itself, a great number of skillful boatmen have come and gone.

Ar, or "black," was the name given to the great Nile by ancient Egyptians. The name was derived from its black-like water colored both by silt carried down from the rich Ethiopian highlands and other dark sediments that come from far upstream on this life-giving river, which extends down over 4,150 miles of the African continent.

The Ar carried a large caravan of sailing vessels and traders yearly from a thousand miles south of the Nile Delta north to the Mediterranean Sea and, in later centuries, far beyond that to distant lands.

Egyptian Sailing Boat

As he peers across the river at the setting sun, the official starter remains as still as the acacia tree in a blazing summer when it seems the wind and all traces of weather, save the oppressive heat, have forsaken this desert land, when the woven papyrus sail is nowhere to be seen along the Ar.

Today promised ideal conditions, however, and the villagers took this to mean their gods looked down upon them with favor. A northeasterly swept across the north-flowing Ar at approximately a 40-degree angle. The sailing would be good.

The sun is three-quarters below the horizon. It can't be long now.

"Give the signal now. The sun is down," an impassioned spectator advises the starter. He does not flinch.

Despite such admonishments to start the contest from many in the crowd who are equally enthusiastic for these races, the sun has not set until the starter says it is so and the event will not begin otherwise. It has been that way for three generations.

One of the day's boatmen, who hails from the most southerly of these villages, about two days by foot, stands alertly in his boat. His dark eyes are on the move, first to the neatly trimmed papyrus sail before him, then proudly down at his vessel, rough-hewn of the acacia tree, and finally, confidently toward the riverbank at the starter. The boatman's skin is the color of the moist earth at the water's edge. As he stands there waiting with his sweep-pole in hand, his long and slender frame seems ill-matched with such powerful arms, but he is fortunate to have limbs like these for they are useful in contests such as these.

His opponent, a local product, stands ankle-deep in his tightly woven, reed vessel, about midway between the stern and mast with its sails formed of animal skins. It is crude by

11

later standards, but a work of ingenuity and great craftsmanship in the eyes of the onlookers. He surveys the riverbank, now teeming with friends and relatives, but also hundreds of strangers. They do not notice that his copper shoulders have grown dull, a sign the race is at hand.

At this moment it seems the Ar is more alive than it has ever been, its people as happy as any. Children squirm from their mothers' grasps as they seek to cool their feet and splash a bit in the inviting water.

Men discuss the attributes of each boatman, and remark at the river's early rise this year and whether it portends harsh times during the days of rain that will come soon. Some lay wagers, but only with things of naught. Others recall their own boating adventures on the Ar.

Women, too, speak of the race, of the handsome contenders and of the day when their sons will set sail on the Ar. They wonder secretly what it would be like to move across the surface of the water in these boats.

Suddenly, there is universal acknowledgement that the sun has set. All eyes turn to the starter. His raised head begins to bow. Yes, that is the signal. They were off and racing on the Ar!

. . . .

In the beginning — long before recorded history — it was a log, perhaps a branch or some sort of debris floating within reach of a human in a river or lake and, for one reason or another, he took hold of it or climbed aboard and away they went, man and vessel forever united.

As the force of current or wind moved the ancient vessel

along, the man — or it could just as well have been a woman or a child — marveled at the wonder and potential of this new invention.

Travel on the land had long since been fairly mastered by humans using their feet, horses and other animals, but water had not been conquered. Moving in the water was a great chore, even if one could swim, and it was so time-consuming. Often, getting to the other side of a lake meant walking a considerable distance, and it was too dangerous to cross wide rivers, which for so long stood as great barriers between regions of peoples.

This floating thing, however, could ease such hardships and open up horizons not yet dreamt of. The notion of traveling great distances by routes other than overland had been inconceivable. Man likely dreamed of flying like the wonderful birds long before he took that first voyage aboard a rudimentary boat. After merely hanging onto a crude craft for many years, the ancient mariner discovered that his hands and arms could be employed to paddle along in the water, and this knowledge would soon lead to the oar.

It was a painstaking, long process for ancient man to construct a boat. He used the stone ax and the adz. Some charred out the center section of a log.

One of the earliest oars probably was a branch still full with the leaves of late spring or summer and eventually this would become a sail. It would not have taken too many voyages before the boatman, who by now had probably advanced to a hollowed-out log or bunches of reeds or vines to form a raft, held the oar branch aloft in a stiff breeze and became excited at the acceleration of his craft. He had become a sailor, but his boat was not designed for such speed and he may have became

Roman Merchant

the first "man overboard" as he went down into the drink. Like any good sailor worth his salt, he probably got back on immediately and tried again.

Hundreds of years passed in each area of the globe where the discovery of travel under sail had been made. New generations each made contributions that improved boats and sails until the day when sailing ships became part of their ways of life.

There came a day when one brave soul set sail to breeze on the open and forbidding sea for the first great voyage of mankind. This sailor was of an ilk that inspired Horace to write, "His heart was mailed with oak and triple brass who first committed a frail ship to the wild seas."

Now with a true sailing vessel that could withstand a rough

trip or two, those in a village who were fortunate enough to learn the art of sailing became boat fishermen and eventually sea merchants, cargo carriers. Some started taxi or ferry services.

The Egyptians and Chinese were among the earliest peoples to build boats capable of traveling long distances over rough seas. Sailors along the great Nile River constructed acacia-wood boats, the forerunners of the present-day caravel types. Their boats were set together brick-fashion, reinforced with inner frames and caulked with papyrus. Sometime around 6,000 B.C., a single woven papyrus sail was hoisted aloft one of these craft and to the craftsman's great delight heartily embraced the wind's driving force. A long sweep pole kept the boat on course. Eventually, a sturdier linen sail replaced the papyrus sail.

It was in such boats that the Egyptians sailed the Mediterranean Sea and beyond, trading an array of goods such as grain, copper items and linen for gold, ivory, incense and olive oil.

So much a part of their lives were boats, that Egyptians placed murals, replica models and limestone reliefs of them in their tombs as the Pharoahs had with their riches, hoping to enjoy them in the afterlife.

Soon after the dawn of civilization, boats of varying sizes and materials were constructed by peoples in numerous regions of the world.

Probably some time after the Egyptians and Chinese discovered boats, the Malay tribes of southeastern Asia as well as other Pacific area peoples discovered they could hop from island to island on boats of reeds and sticks bundled and fastened together.

Reed boats also were built by Bolivian and Peruvian Indians high in the Andes Mountains on Lake Titicaca, which has many reed islands across its great expanse. After learning to build these boats — you can still watch them do it today — the Indians then began to live on the reed islands, a practice many continue. Their boats, some with huts, are not unlike those used a thousand or more years ago.

Native peoples in other lands also continue boat-building traditions learned long ago. Many still use bark, natural matted materials or animal hides.

American Indians and Australian Aborigines each separately invented bark canoes.

People in several corners of the world learned early that the hides of animals could be used to cover and greatly reinforce their boats. The finest skin-covered boats in the world are the umiak and kayak of the Alaskan and Canadian Eskimo.

Sails over the millenia also have been fashioned from a variety of materials, including papyrus, woven grass, fiber, flax, hides, cotton and nylon.

The Phoenicians perhaps were the most masterful seafarers of antiquity. Unlike many of their predecessors, these sailors did not have to hug coastlines or sail solely by day because they learned to navigate according to tables of distances and the natural and unchanging routes of the stars.

These former desert nomads, who merely continued their wanderings at sea, came into prominence as the Egyptian Empire waned. They settled the eastern shore of the Mediterranean and started the ports of Tyre, Sidon and Biblos. They invented galleys, called biremes, with high sides that held two rows of oars on each side. These galleys were shallow-draft, 70 feet long and carried linen and wool cloth, jewelry made by Phoenician craftsmen and the purple-black dye only the wealthy could afford. The Phoenicians were able to sail afar by virtue of their fine vessels, which were the envy of other peoples whose ships were not yet so reliable. In the British Isles, they traded for tin from Cornwall, in Asia Minor for wine and in Greece for pottery. They also dealt in slave trade.

In 878 B.C., Phoenicians colonized Carthage in North Africa where there had existed a long trade rivalry between Greece and Rome. Roman soldiers destroyed that city in 146 B.C., and the Phoenicians and their lands were eventually absorbed into the Roman Empire.

The Greeks bought Phoenician goods, borrowed their alphabet, then learned their trading methods. They learned well and eventually built better ships, surpassing the Phoenicians in sea trade. Success led to the need for warships to protect Greek merchant ships carrying pottery, textiles and metal wares bound for ports where there were grain, fish and other goods for trade.

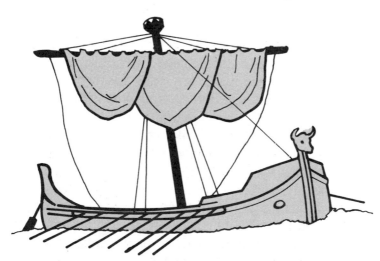

Phoenician Trader

From ancient times to modern the sea has served mankind as a battleground. Ships have been used as tactical vehicles and to transport warriors and weapons. It was for the purpose of battle that the Greeks constructed the trireme, a vessel with a fierce ram, three banks of oars on each side and it was manned by as many as 170 oarsmen. The idea for this ship also probably came from the Phoenicians. The vessel, used extensively as a warship, carried a square sail of woven material. While it was certainly economical to use the sails anytime, galley men were aboard to supply the power when there was a threat of war because they could also be called on to fight. This ship may have made the difference when the Greeks sailed against the Persians in the battle of Salamis in 480 B.C.

Although the motive force of Greco-Roman military ships could come from either sails or oarsmen, the merchant ships of those two nations almost always were powered by sail, except when the wind failed.

In the 9th century B.C., when sailing ships were the workhorses of international trade, it was the adventure and romance of a sea voyage, the wind lashing the sails that captured the attention of Homer, who wrote, "But soon an off-shore breeze blew to our liking, a canvas-bellying breeze . . . The bows went plunging . . . sails cracked and lashed out."

For centuries Greece enjoyed its Golden Age, at sea as well as on land, but by 300 B.C. Rome and Carthage had achieved superiority at sea over all nations.

The vastness of the Roman Empire led her armies to construct an incredible number of roads and bridges to control it. These roads and bridges are recorded as being among the colossal feats of the ancient world, but the Romans also undertook to establish 50,000 miles of ocean highways as well to maintain its stronghold. To achieve this, two types of boats were built: One was a fast, highly maneuverable galley intended for fighting and patrolling; The other, a commercial boat, was slow and it was fat, but it never tired — as the Greek poet Hesiod wrote, "Praise a slim ship, but put your goods in a fat one."

The Roman merchant ship, which usually had just two banks of oars because space was needed for cargo and passengers, depended on the wind for power and therefore always carried sails. In the building of these ships, a mortise and tenon type of construction was used to make the craft watertight.

As the Roman Empire declined so, too, did the quality of her ships, and fewer ships were turned out in Rome, a city in which shipbuilding had been big business for centuries.

Far to the north, about or before the 7th century A.D., the legendary Vikings were sailing in ships with rudimentary keels. Findings indicate their boats had improved greatly by the following century. What had been a small piece of cloth had grown into a large, square sail, like that of a craft found on the Swedish island of Gotland. The Viking sail, a striped, red and blue or plain blood-red, was feared by all. It was loose-footed — not attached to a spar at the foot or base of this typically double-ended ship, which was similar to vessels sailed by other Northern European nations.

Some variations of the Vikings' clinker-built Gokstad ship may have been used as pleasure vessels, while a longer model was typical of the warships these Norsemen used to raid the coasts of Northern Europe in the 9th and 10th centuries. The sides of these boats, with overlapping planks similar to boats still widely used, could be increased in height, especially for carrying cargo. In addition to a keel used for balance and stability, there was a long, large rudder that was swung by a

Viking Long Ship

tiller. Holes were cut in the sides for 16 oars. A rack along the sides was used to display the round shields of the warriors on board. The Vikings were fearless in battle and they were quite adept at handling their "long ships." Prior to 1,000 a.d. they apparently were able to sail them to wind, or at less than a 90-degree angle to the wind.

Viking ships were slow to change, however, and the trading vessels of other nations where there had been advancements in design began to outdistance the ships to the north. The long ships were slow in comparison and had to be beached for unloading while the use of quays elsewhere sped up the process, rendering the Viking vessels less competitive.

Despite their passing, the Vikings left their mark on the world. So feared for centuries were they that the nations of Northern Europe were forced to organize navies and engage in shipbuilding to protect themselves. William the Conqueror and his army stormed the coast of England in single-masted ships similar to those of the Vikings. In 1066 following his victory in the Battle of Hastings he went on to become England's first Norman king.

To the south, the much larger, two-three-and four-masted Mediterranean ships were superior to those in use throughout Northern Europe. In the 12th century, about the time the compass came into use, Genoese vessels had two decks, three in the 13th century. The finest sails — they were the long, tapered lateen style — were manufactured either in Genoa or Marseilles. Planks were sealed with pitch and fitted together edge to edge instead of by overlapping them as builders were doing in the north.

Steerage was about the only area in which Mediterranean sailing ships were inferior to those of the north. The stern rudder did not appear in the south until the 14th century. Instead, a pair of lateral rudders, one on each side of the stern, were used to steer.

Only the Chinese junk, news of which was brought to Europe by Marco Polo in the 13th and early 14th centuries, was comparable to the best Mediterranean sailing ship, though Westerners thought it was awkward-looking. In the 9th century, about the time the Vikings enjoyed naval supremacy in the waters of Northern Europe, there were dozens of types of these Chinese junks, which are considered to be some of the most efficient sailing vessels in the world. They had from one to five masts. Junk sails are a series of matted or linen panels connected

21

to the masts in such a way that they can all be close-hauled, allowing the boat to sail closer into the wind than other types of sailing ships.

Many nations went into the ship-building business at the height of the Renaissance and vessels rapidly began to improve in many respects. Instrument makers and sailors, like Portugal's Prince Henry the Navigator, were improving navigation aids in the 14th and 15th centuries; the astrolabe, used to measure the altitude of the sun and stars, was largely replaced with the cross-staff. The lateen sail greatly improved sailing efficiency and was widely used in the 15th century; while some ships maintained all square sails, others combined those with lateen sails and still others went to strictly lateen sails.

Financed by the king and queen of Spain, an Italian navigator by the name of Cristoforo Colon set sail in 1492 in search of the East Indies to prove to himself and the world that the earth was round, a very unpopular notion at the time. On his long voyage that took him to the new world Cristopher Columbus helmed the "Santa Maria," the 100-foot sailer that was the flagship of his fleet of three. The great voyages of Columbus, Amerigo Vespucci, Vasco da Gama, Sir Francis Drake and many other explorers and navigators during this rich age of exploration via the seas coincided with and spawned technical advancement in ships and shipbuilding, which by this period was heartily promoted and funded by governments seeking to lay claim to distant new lands and riches.

There had been extensive trade across the seas for centuries, but the 1,600s saw seafaring nations engaged as never before in heated competition for that trade. That competition precipitated new boat styles, two in particular: One was the English-designed frigate with its low bow and stern designed specifically for battle at sea, so it had to be rugged, but it also had to be swift in order to maintain the trade edge; The other was the yacht and was intended mainly for pleasure and racing.

The pleasure boat was not new. There are historical accounts of Roman and Greek royalty and court dignitaries owning boats for personal transportation and racing. In the 1st century B.C. Cleopatra often lounged in her personal luxurious barge. Wealthy Chinese had their "flower boats." The Dutch are believed to have been the first to engage extensively in boat racing for sport — that was during the 16th and 17th centuries — though their boats bore no resemblance to today's sleek and speedy yachts.

The word, yacht, comes from the Dutch word for a type of boat known as the "jachtschiff" or "jaghtschip," a light, swift, sailing sloop, often used to run down pirate ships.

The sport of yachting, by many accounts, had its modern beginnings at the time of the English Restoration in 1660 when the monarchy, defunct for several years, and royal lands were restored. Parliament accepted Charles II that year as the rightful monarch and later that same year the Dutch presented him with a gift, the yacht, *Mary*. Twenty years later, Charles, who was known to have laid a wager on a boat race, defeated the Duke of York and a Dutch entry in one of earliest recorded contests. Sailing enthusiast that he was, Charles initiated a tradition of royal patronage toward such contests.

Many yacht owners had entered their boats in small, private contests around Europe for some time, but yacht clubs and organized yacht racing didn't come about until the early 18th century. The oldest known club, the Cork Water Club of Ireland (now the Royal Cork Yacht Club), organized in 1720. The Cumberland Fleet, predecessor to the Royal Thames Yacht Club,

Greek Sailer

was formed in 1775 in England.

In 1749 what was believed to be the first formal race was held on the Thames River in England. Competition at the time was was limited to two boats.

Yacht racing also was emerging about this time in America where yachts were being modeled after commercial pilot boats. Yachting already had been a popular pastime in the American colonies in the early 1700s, at least for those who could afford the time to sail and the expense of a boat. The Knickerbocker

Boat Club of New York formed in 1811, but like so many others during the period, it was short-lived.

While many clubs formed and folded during this period particular attention was being paid to the yachts themselves, at making them luxurious at the expense of efficiency. This continued throughout most of the 19th century when sailboat racing was becoming fairly common. So while the races were at times highly competitive and the participants emotional, there were always provisions on board for a spot of tea or something a little stronger.

By the turn of the century, yacht construction in America was in full swing, especially with one Eastern family. From the banks of the Hudson River across from New York there came a well-known figure in early American yachting history, John C. Stevens, of Hoboken, N.J. Together with his brother Edwin, who was equally renowned in the sport, he built the 20-foot sailboat, *Diver*, in 1809. That was followed in 1816 by *Trouble*, a 56-footer, and then in 1820 by *Double Trouble*, a boat believed to have been the first catamaran built in America.

John Stevens' *Wave*, which measured 65 feet at the waterline and 72 feet from bow to stern, went head to head in August 1835 with George Crowninshield's schooner, *Sylph*, in a race that may have been the first yacht race in America.

Yacht racing gradually was emerging elsewhere in the world during the 19th century.

Two years after the *Wave-Sylph* race, what is now the Royal Nova Scotia Squadron in Canada, where sailing and yachting had been popular for many decades, was organized as the Halifax Yacht Club, the oldest yacht club in North America. In 1860 the Prince of Wales, who later was crowned King Edward VII, became the club's patron and presented it with the Prince of Wales Cup. The club had applied to Queen Victoria for "royal" status and with the prince's endorsement was granted the title, Royal Halifax Yacht Club. After some difficult years over the next two decades — there was a membership split and a tragic race in which three lives were lost — the club reunited and became known by its present name, the Royal Nova Scotia Yacht Squadron. In honor of Queen Victoria's jubilee celebration in 1887, the club held its first race for the cup. In 1905 it sponsored the Halifax Race, the first ocean race from America to Canada. The squadron boasts a royal patronage extending from King George V to Prince Philip, Duke of Edinburgh.

In Australia where most of the people have resided in coastal areas throughout the nation's history, sailboat races have been run for more than 100 years. The Royal Sydney Yacht Squadron was established in 1862.

In 1879 an assemblage of yachting enthusiasts was taking place in a nation that had been under sail since before the ancient Etruscans had stepped on its shores. It was a nation where the construction of sailing ships had developed into an art. This was the first meeting of the Regio Yacht Club Italiano, which drew up its rules the following year.

Back to Stevens. One of his brothers, Robert, put his engineering expertise to work to settle the popular dispute over whether the keel or centerboard was most advantageous in racing. He incorporated in his design comparative pre-testing of two scale models, a practice still in use today. In 1846 he designed the *Maria*, a boat equipped with modern features such as a hollow boom and crosscut sails. On June 30, 1844, two years before *Maria* was built, the New York Yacht Club was organized on board another Stevens boat, the schooner, *Gimcrack*.

While the Stevens family and others turned out better and better boats every year for pleasure and for racing, most of the sloops, schooners and frigates in existence were utilized as they always had been, to be the workhorses of long-distance trade. They ran the Hudson daily, crossed the Atlantic and sailed to and from far-off India for tea and other goods that were in great demand.

More than a quarter-century before the Stevens brothers came into prominence in the industry, the end already was in sight for what had surely been the golden age of sailing ships on the international trading scene. Jacques Perier's steam-powered boat was successfully tested in 1775 and soon steam would be commonplace. Sailing ships persisted for another 100 years on the trade scene, but by the late 19th century they had been relegated largely to their current status, as vessels of sport and recreation. That's not to say the seas play host only to racers and recreational sailors. Classic-style sailing ships throughout the world still serve as traders while others are used for a variety of purposes, including as training craft for the naval personnel of many nations.

Despite the dwindling use of sailing ships in world trade, it must be remembered that for more than 7,000 years they reigned supreme in trade and those vessels powered by other means in contrast are barely 200 years old.

Fairs and exhibitions held in the 1800s by countries seeking to promote their products in the international marketplace were likely to attract a shipbuilder or designer now and then. Such an event was slated to open May 1, 1851. The Great London Exhibition was billed as the first international exhibition. The Englishman, Joseph Paxton, designed a glass and iron building covering 21 acres in Hyde Park for the purpose of hosting the very finest in the world's arts and sciences. U.S. businessmen packed up their goods and sailed across the Atlantic to display them at the exhibition. Samuel Colt brought the new mass-produced revolver that bore his name. Cyrus McCormick went to England seeking new markets for his revolutionary reaper. Gail Borden was awarded a gold medal for his meat biscuits, and Edward Corliss displayed his version of the sailing ship's Nemesis, a 2,500 horsepower steam engine.

In all, the exhibition reportedly drew an astounding 6 million visitors, including a 170-ton, 100-foot schooner that would be the first to compete in what was to become sailing's greatest race. Her construction was financed in 1851 by the newly formed syndicate of John and Edwin Stevens, George Schuyler, Col. James A. Hamilton, Hamilton Wilkes and J.K.B. Finlay.

Before the year was out, events would ensure that international yacht racing would be at full sail and downwind. Today it appears that rather than being at its end, sailing is more popular than ever and millions of people around the world now enjoy yacht racing.

Chapter II

America's Cup History

When the New York Yacht Club decided in late 1851 to finance the construction of a boat to represent America at the Great London Exhibition the following spring, the members had it in mind to prove to England, considered then to be the dominant power in yacht racing and design, that Yankee know-how could compete with the best.

Shipbuilder William H. Brown was greatly impressed with a model for the yacht, so much so that he was sure such a boat could beat any British vessel of similar size. If it couldn't, he informed his friend, now Commodore John Stevens, and the New York Yacht Club, he'd build the boat for nothing.

Stevens and others had believed for some time that Yankee boats were as good or better than any in the world. Long before this, he and his brothers had been spoiling for an international race, and the *Onkahye*, built in 1839, may originally have been intended for such a purpose.

American and English boats already had competed against each other prior to 1851 but not in formal races. They'd been doing some very long-distance racing from England to China and back. The British Navigation Act forbidding foreign vessels from docking in British ports with cargo was repealed in 1848, and American ship owners seized the opportunity to compete with the English for tea and other goods in Chinese Ports. Frequently, those who docked first did the best trade, like Theodore Palmer's ship, the *Oriental*, which made a haul from Hong Kong to England in 97 days, trimming 18 days off the existing record. That sent a wave of fear through English shipping companies. To drive the point home, the American Navigation Club once offered a purse of 10,000 pounds for a cargo race from England to China, proposing to pit a ship built and manned by the British against a ship built and manned by Americans. There were no takers, not even when the prize was doubled and a large headstart was offered to the British. Merchants gave American clippers the best tonnage fees and the faster American ships also liked the British practice of giving a bonus to the first tea-bearing ship to dock each year.

These were the days of the big Baltimore clipper ships, but when steam came along boat builders began constructing similar, but smaller, leaner and swifter craft, such as the English tea clipper. These boats reduced even more the time for hauling tea to England, but soon they were bound for other pastures as well — the gold fields of California in 1849 and Australia in 1851. (In the fall of 1986 yachtsmen and their sailing ships also docked in an Australian port with equal fervor.)

Somewhere, someone was always turning out a faster clipper, but ship owners and captains in America and elsewhere learned to deal with that.

What they could not deal with around the turn of the 19th century was a new type of motive force, one that could drive a boat over water even when its sails lay limp. Unbelieving New Yorkers dubbed Robert Fulton's steamship, *Fulton's Folly*, while it was under construction in their city, but the ridicule was silenced in August 1807 when the *Clermont* steamed 150 miles up the Hudson in the unprecedented time of 32 hours. Soon riverboats were racing one another on the Ohio, Mississippi and other inland waterways. Combining steam and sail in 1819, the *Savannah*, a sailing ship equipped with a steam engine, crossed the Atlantic in 25 days. Debarking in Savannah, Geo., and docking in London, it was the first time a vessel had crossed the ocean using steam. The first true steamer, built in England by engineer Isambard K. Brunel, took 14 days to get from Bristol, England to New York.

Despite the advent of the steamer, the sailing ship remained in the forefront of overseas trade for much of the rest of the century. Though it gradually lost the competitive edge in that realm, it had survived the whole of civilized history and was not now near the "bitter end." Smaller cutters, schooners, sloops and yachts all were gaining in prominence by the mid-1800s as boats of recreation and pleasure and as implements of sport. As long as there is a breeze and someone left to challenge the sea armed only with a sail, sailing ships are likely to go on surviving.

Men like Stevens, it has been noted, were seeking some big-time racing and men like his friend, George Steers, one of the period's premier designers of fast schooners, had the skill to provide him with the best boats to do it. Having previously worked with the Stevens brothers, Steers' capability was known, so it was natural for the New York Yacht Club to approach him. They asked him in late 1850 to make a model of a boat they wanted to send over to England. He accepted. Steers coincidentally had the time to devote to the project because the shipbuilding firm of which he'd been a partner had gone out of business the previous year. Despite the original features of many of his earlier designs, the model Steers produced in 1851 was not terribly innovative. Certainly the boat was fast, as subsequent events would prove, but it was never tried against what were considered to be the fastest boats of the time. Features of Steers' model, the hollow-hull design and its main beam placed abaft the middle among others, probably had been borrowed from other boats. He had selected the best features of the day.

The black schooner that resulted from his labors was known as the *America*, and she was destined to be revered by thousands of sailors around the world for more than a century and who knows how much longer. Her story is at the heart of yacht-racing lore. Construction of the schooner took less than three months, but the *America* wasn't completed in time for the May 1st start of the London Exhibition. In a test run against the *Maria*, designed by Robert Stevens, she fared poorly and was held back for modifications. On June 18, she was delivered to her owners at a revised cost of $20,000. Fine lines and bows like hers that weren't so full were on the rise at the time but after the *America* they were the trend. Her bow was narrow and pointed, she weighed 170 tons and, give or take a little, she measured 100 feet.

The *America* set sail June 21 for Europe under the command of renowned Sandy Hook pilot Dick Brown. He crossed the Atlantic in 30 days, docking in the French seaport of Le Havre at the mouth of the Seine River. There the schooner was refitted and cleaned up and then it was northwest across the English Channel for the Isle of Wight and, Stevens hoped, a little racing. It's not certain as she approached the southern coast of England whether it had already been decided to enter the craft in what was to be the first international cup race, the Royal Yacht Squadron Regatta. There is a strong possibility Stevens had this in mind.

With a rakish look about her, the *America* arrived at the seaport city of Cowes about Aug. 1, amid a wave of speculation and some disbelief over her potentcy because she encountered her escort miles out in the Solent and beat her handily.

All eyes were upon her as she sailed in effortlessly, or so it seemed to the inhabitants of Cowes' waterfront homes. News of the encounter spread quickly, and it shocked many, though some took it less seriously. The yachting community, however, was sufficiently impressed.

The commodore's propensity for a wager had not been satisfied by this mere chance dash to port so he offered up to 10,000 guineas for a race between the pride of the Yankees and any British vessel. There would be no race because there were no takers. The British press quickly jumped all over the home contingent and there was some feeling among the members of the squadron that the "Race of All Nations," as it was dubbed, would give them an opportunity to redeem themselves on the home front.

Stevens entered the *America* in the regatta when it appeared she might be relegated to a status of merely showing off her trim lines but never proving them. The week before the regatta, the *America* ran a short stretch of the course on which she would race.

"She went along very steadily and well up to Ryde," the London Times reported, "but she did not show any great superiority till she was off the pier . . . when she seemed as if she had put a screw into her stern, hoisted her fore and aft foresail sail, and began to fly through the water. She passed schooners and cutters one after the other just as a Derby winner passes the 'ruck,' and as the breeze freshened slid with the speed of an arrow out towards the Nab, standing upright as a ramrod under her canvas . . . She went about in splendid style, a little short of the Nab, spinning around like a top, and came bowling away toward Cowes as fast if not faster than ever. As if to let our best craft see she did not care about them, the *America* went up to each in succession, ran to leeward of every one of them as close as she could, and shot before them in succession, coming to achor at Ryde at least two miles, as it seemed to me, ahead of any of the craft she had been running against."

The following week she and 14 British vessels, eight cutters and six schooners, awaited the signal to start the Royal Yacht Squadron Regatta. The Hundred Guineas Cup, which has survived to become the most sought-after prize in international yacht racing, awaited the victor of the regatta, a 53-mile course around the Isle of Wight.

It was not an auspicious start the morning of Aug. 22, 1851, for the *America*. Her sails had been hoisted before her anchor had been weighed and she slued awhile in place. When she finally got off, trailing the pack, it took her a while to catch a breeze that would enable her to make some headway.

This race was far from over, and Capt. Brown set about the business of maneuvering in the unfamiliar water which had certain quirks known to favor the home crews.

Brown was a fine sailor. He soon sailed back into contention, and not to his surprise but to the dismay of the others in the regatta, he was able to run by them with the greatest of ease. They were powerless in the game because their boats were no match for this one.

The *America* sailed along for a time without incident, comfortably in front. Suddenly, just before 1 p.m., her jib boom snapped while sailing into the wind. She was able to manage

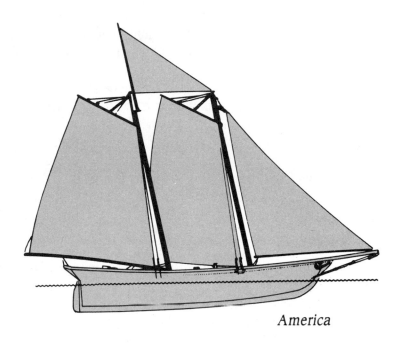

America

and it didn't matter anyway, because the upstart schooner already had built a substantial lead and could not be overtaken while she made adjustments.

After the boats rounded the island and were out of sight, there was little for the spectators to do but wait. They were anxious to know: Was it a British boat or the American in the lead?

One such inquiry came from none other than Queen Victoria just as there appeared a lone boat in the distance.

"Who is first?" the queen inquired of her attendant.

To the attendant's reply that it was the *America*, she further inquired, "Oh indeed, and which is second?"

To this second inquiry by her grace, the attendant replied in words that ring true to every sailor who has tried and failed to win the cup: "Madam, there is no second."

The *America* was not daunted by the delay the boom break had caused and late in the day ghosted over the finish line with most of the competition well out of sight behind her. At the contest's end, in the twilight of the day when spectators surely must have been weary and anxious to retire to their homes, the cup was lost. Formal protests from five of the competitors alleging the Yankee cutter had strayed illegally inside course limits were denied. Her eight-minute victory was enough that under the scoring system *America* probably would have remained the victor had the protests been upheld.

Although British yachtsmen were smarting considerably after the ordeal, the grace that was Queen Victoria's overshadowed their dour moods. She paid Stevens, the other syndicate members, Brown and the rest of the crew the royal honor they were due and presented them with the 27-inch high cup forged of 8.4 pounds of silver, an inconsequential monetary value compared to the prestige the trophy symbolized then and ever since.

The Cup journeyed to its new home across the Atlantic but Stevens sold her future namesake.

As for the ship that has perhaps been the most well-known yacht around the world, she was to go through a succession of owners, one of whom changed her name to *Camilla*. *America* found her way home again and went on to serve both the Union and Confederate armies during the Civil War. For the North she was a naval dispatch ship and training vessel. For the South she was a blockade runner, her speed and light draft enabling her to slip through Northern lines carrying medical and military supplies.

On her golden anniversary in 1901, the feisty little ship that won the silver cup went into retirement following a New York Yacht Club regatta. A group of citizens later restored the *America* and presented her to the U.S. Naval Academy. In 1946 the aging matron of the America's Cup race, held 16 times since she started it all 95 years before, sadly, was broken up.

Members of the syndicate passed the Cup around until 1857 when they donated it permanently to the New York Yacht Club, stipulating in a "Deed of Gift" that friendly nations compete for the Cup periodically. Each competing nation was obligated to construct its own vessel and provide its own crew as well as sail it on its own bottom to the site of the race, the deed stipulated.

Eventually, people began referring to the trophy as the America's Cup.

Despite the invitation to other nations to take the Cup if they could, the first challenge didn't come until 19 years after *America's* historic run around Wight.

1870
Magic vs. Cambria

The American yacht, *Sappho*, designed by William Townsend, didn't compete in the first Cup challenge but it did play an important role in bringing the contest about. The owners of the British schooners, *Cambria* and *Aline*, offered to race the *Sappho*, which had gone to England in search of a buyer.

It was perhaps an untimely decision because the *Sappho* reportedly was still in her cruising rig and improperly ballasted, not optimum conditions for a race. But race she did and the

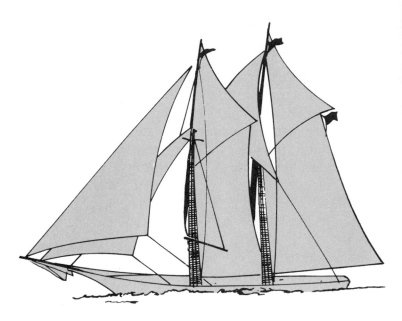

Schooner-Yacht SAPPHO

Cambria won handily. *Cambria's* owner, James Ashbury, was so pleased he issued a challenge for the Cup to the New York Yacht Club, which accepted.

In an attempt to simulate the conditions of the 1851 race, the *Cambria* was required to sail on her own bottom to the United States where she would race against a fleet of sailers representing the New York Yacht Club.

Among the club's entries was the *Magic*, designed by Philadelphian, Richard Loper, along the lines of the "sandbagger," sloops and catamarans measuring 18-28 feet in length. These sandbaggers raced under a length rule and were first popular in the mid-1850s in New York waters.

Built by the New York firm, Byerly and Son, she was first launched in 1857 under the name, *Madgie*. Loper modified *Madgie* considerably in 1859, giving her a new stern and converting her to a schooner. Her bow was lengthened in 1860 and four years later she was sold.

Her new owner renamed her *Magic*, and entered the vessel in her first race with the New York Yacht Club in 1865. The year before the first Cup challenge *Magic* was completely rebuilt. Although schooners of her type had a bad reputation, her modifications over the years had left her a speedy and seaworthy craft in 1870 for her newest owner Franklin Osgood. *Magic* is precisely what she was when she went up against the *Cambria* and 16 American boats whose owners hoped to win the trophy. She easily defeated them all in a one-race contest. *Magic* went on to become a pilot boat and a supply boat for many years.

Even if Ashbury didn't win the race, two things were clear: Some Englishmen wanted the Cup back home ''where it belonged;'' and there apparently did exist some interest for holding periodic international runs for the prize as proposed in the Deed of Gift.

1871
Columbia and Sappho vs. Livonia

Again the challenger came from England and her name was *Livonia*. Her owner was Ashbury, back for another shot in a best-of-four series. Following complaints that the Americans had an unfair advantage, the New York Yacht Club decided the *Livonia* would only have to race against a single boat. Retaining a little extra advantage, however, the club also ruled that since multiple races were planned it would choose which defender to race each day. That of course would depend on the weather.

The *Columbia*, designed by Joseph Van Deusen and owned by Osgood, was fairly new and exceptionally fast when she beat the *Livonia* two out three races.

Sappho finally made it to Cup competition for the last two races of the 1871 series against the *Livonia*, which had no better luck against her, losing twice. *Sappho*, redesigned by her new owner, William P. Douglas, atoned for her thrashing by the *Cambria* years before. It was probably undeserved because then she had raced ill-prepared. She had proved her self this time, however, and in fact was now considered to be the fastest keel boat in America.

1876
Madeleine vs. Countess of Dufferin

If it seemed England and America would race each other forever in what was supposed to be an international contest, the notion died when a new nation, Canada, came on the scene. In the 1876 competition, the New York Yacht Club made another move toward greater fairness and decided that the challenger would face only one boat, and whichever yacht was selected must be equal to the weather each racing day. *Madeleine* was a sloop converted into a schooner. Owned by John S. Dickerson, she won 2-0 in a best-of-three series over Canada's *Countess of Dufferin*, owned by Charles Gifford. It was such a poor showing, Toronto's Royal Canadian Yacht Club may have wished it had kept the *Countess* at home and let the British try again.

1881
Mischief vs. Atalanta

Following an 1876 disaster in which the shallow-hulled yacht, *Mohawk*, capsized at anchor and her owner and several guests drowned, the *Mischief* was built with safety in mind.

Mischief was constructed with a deeper hull, broader beam and lower ballast placement than vessels like the *Mohawk*. These features gave the boat greater stability. Combined with a double headsail rig, *Mischief* defeated another Canadian challenger, *Atalanta*, 2-0 in another two-of-three matchup. Ontario's Bay of Quinte Yacht Club in Belleville had entered the sloop and its failure combined with that of the *Countess of Dufferin* in the previous Cup match prompted the New York Yacht Club to rewrite the rules and eliminate all freshwater challengers. That meant challenges from those clubs and organizations using the Great Lakes and similar inland bodies of water for sailing would not be accepted. They would be prohibited from vying for the Cup.

1885
Puritan vs. Genesta

Boats like the Scottish cutter, *Madge*, which had beat many centerboard yachts, impressed designer Edward Burgess, a Harvard-educated naturalist who may have drawn ideas from it for the cutter, *Puritan*. The *Puritan* was a compromise boat that satisfied the proponents of shoal centerboards and narrow cutters. It had a deep centerboard. *Puritan* owners J.M. Forbes and Gen. Charles Paine were pleased enough with the 1885

Cup defender. The *Puritan* defeated England's *Genesta*, owned by Sir Richard Sutton, 2-0 in the last two-out-of-three series to be held in Cup competition.

1886
Mayflower vs. Galatea

Paine returned in 1886 with the *Mayflower*, another of Burgess' designs, and won 2-0 over Lt. William Henn's *Galatea*, of England.

1887
Volunteer vs. Thistle

Three years before Burgess died in 1891, *Volunteer* became the third yacht designed by him to win the America's Cup. *Volunteer* defeated *Thistle* of Scotland 2-0. In all, Burgess, who had only taken up design as a hobby in England and later yacht design professionally, turned out a remarkable 137 boats. He left a lasting influence on American yachts as well as the Cup race.

1893
Vigilant vs. Valkyrie II

Two newcomers to the America's Cup scene this year were boat designer Nat Herreshoff for the defense and the Earl of Dunraven for England. Herreshoff combined the keel and centerboard concepts and the result was *Vigilant*, which did away with Dunraven's *Valkyrie II* 3-0.

1895
Defender vs. Valkyrie III

Defender was another Herreshoff design. It had a deep, sharp hull with manganese bronze and aluminum plating that eventually corroded. There was 85 tons of lead ballast in her keel to keep her stable in the wind. Dunraven was back again and after being skunked 3-0 a second time (he withdrew from the third race) he submitted several allegations, including that *Defender's* waterline was illegal and her ballast had been shifted contrary to the rules. Additionally, he contended that the spectator fleet had hampered his sailing. The protests were reviewed and rejected. It was common practice after a denial that the accuser apologize, but Dunraven felt he'd been treated unfairly and no apology was issued.

1899
Columbia vs. Shamrock I

Four years after Dunraven's failed bid there appeared on the scene a man from Scotland who won the hearts of those on both sides of the Atlantic, not only with his tea but also with a graciousness, good humor and a brand of sportsmanship that made competing for the America's Cup a pleasure for all.

Sir Thomas Lipton — the title was bestowed on him in 1898 for his efforts on behalf of working class people — wanted the Cup badly and would seek it with an unrivaled tenacity for 31 years. Lipton, who made his fortune primarily in the tea business, began his quest in 1899 with the first of five boats in the *Shamrock* line. *Shamrock I* went up against *Columbia* another Herreshoff boat owned by financier J.P. Morgan and C.O. Iselin. Perhaps the most exciting aspect of the series — *Columbia* whipped *Shamrock I* 3-0 — was that the New York Herald reported the race over a radio transmission from the *S.S. Ponce* at 15 words per minute.

1901
Columbia vs. Shamrock II

Two years later Lipton returned with *Shamrock II* to face *Columbia* once again.

Boston yachtsman Thomas J. Lawson had hoped to be the defender of the Cup but wasn't permitted to do so because he didn't belong to the New York Yacht Club. Unable to compete, Lawson instead wrote a book on the subject — Lawson's History of the America's Cup — but he would have preferred living the experience rather than writing about it.

Columbia defeated Shamrock II 3-0.

1903
Reliance vs. Shamrock III

Undaunted in the face of defeat, the persistant Lipton tried again. At least this time he got a new opponent, *Reliance*, but it was another of Herreshoff's winning designs.

Reliance was a fin-keel scow boat, carried 16,600 square feet of sail and despite its massiveness could move through the water at a 7.3-knot clip. Due to the rating rules governing the races prior to 1905, American boats had evolved into a skimming dish style similar to the British boats. The Reliance was the extreme in this style, having an overhang of more than 5 feet and a waterline length of 89 feet, 8 inches.

She was a speedy yacht and defeated Lipton 3-0. Two years after this race the Universal Rule corrected such extremes by establishing the "letter" classes of boats and controlling such items as overhang, draft and freeboard. In 1906 the International Rule established the metered-class boats.

1920
Resolute vs. Shamrock IV

The last of the Herreshoff Cup boats was *Resolute*, built in 1914. World War I erupted that year so Lipton's *Shamrock IV* and *Resolute* were forced to postpone an encounter until 1920. In the 17 years since the last race Lipton and his crew apparently had learned a trick or two, but the Herreshoff touch was too much again. *Resolute* won 3-2. Herreshoff, now America's most well-known and respected designer, retired. Lipton, meanwhile, was so widely associated with the America's Cup, that some waggishly, others quite seriously, referred to it at the "Lipton Cup."

1930
Enterprise vs. Shamrock V

The J-Class yachts marked the races from 1930 through 1937. These yachts had masts as high as 165 feet and measured as long as 80 feet or 24 meters at the water line. Although the name of Herreshoff wouldn't be associated with the 1930 race, that of another well-known designer would. *Enterprise* was designed by W. Starling Burgess, son of Edward Burgess who had designed three cup winners. Despite having his Nemesis of four previous races now in retirement, Lipton again was blanked, this time 4-0 in what had become and remains today a best-of-seven contest. The races that year and through the 1983 matchups were held 30 miles off Newport, R.I. in Rhode Island Sound. In addition to being a Burgess design. *Enterprise*, owned by Harold S. Vanderbilt, had such innovations as a 162-foot Duralumin mast, a flat-top "Park Avenue" boom, which gave the mainsail foot an aerodynamic curve, and below the deck winches run by an eight-man gang. Not only did the Americans have a superior boat, but Vanderbilt and his crew's sailing skills also were top-notch. Of his crew and the yacht, Vanderbilt wrote, "Sailing vessels . . . are a continuing challenge. We learned something, many things, every time we went out, and we went out at every opportunity." Lipton, of course, knew that Vanderbilt and the others he had faced over the years were tough competitors and this one last time, as ever, he accepted his defeat with dignity and good humor. In Lipton the Cup and all of sport had seen one of its finest competitors.

It was the great American humorist, Will Rogers, who suggested to Lipton's followers in the United States that they each donate $1 toward the purchase of a cup to be presented to the grand old man. Admiring Americans raised $16,000 for a gold cup wrought for the warmhearted 80-year-old yachtsman by Tiffany & Co., of New York where it is on display.

Inscribed on the cup are Shamrock leaves representing his yachts and these words: "This symbol of a voluntary outpouring of Love, Admiration and Esteem is Presented to the Gamest Loser in the World of Sport. In the name of the Hundreds of Thousands of Americans and Wellwishers of Sir Thomas Johnstone Lipton Bart, KCVO."

1934
Rainbow vs. Endeavour

Vanderbilt again defended the Cup, but with a new boat, *Rainbow*, another design of the younger Burgess. *Endeavour*, owned by Englishman T.O.M. Sopwith, made a good showing, but was defeated 4-2.

Sopwith and *Rainbow* had posed the greatest threat yet to the New York Yacht Club. He took the first two races. In the fourth he protested twice that *Rainbow* had fouled his boat, but the club wouldn't even consider the matter, contending that he hadn't raised the protest flags promptly enough. Sopwith was livid.

1937
Ranger vs. Endeavour II

Burgess and Olin Stephens combined their talent for the

18th America's Cup competition by designing a defender for Vanderbilt. *Ranger* may have been the fastest yacht to windward yet. It had 7,500 square feet of sail, less than half that of *Reliance*, the 1903 defender, but *Ranger's* average sailing speed during the 1937 contest, 7.8 knots, was about one-half knot faster. Design changes enabled *Ranger* to garner greater speed despite less sail. The smaller, flatter spinnakers of earlier days were gone. *Ranger* carried a huge 18,000 square-foot, parachute-shaped spinnaker that provided extra pulling power. Sopwith's second *Endeavour* was no match in the end for *Ranger*. He lost 4-0 but the races were recorded as having been well fought.

Ranger

The end of the series marked the beginning of the longest span between races. In the interim, World War II had gripped the planet, a war had split Korea and the space and computer age had dawned. It was the end of an era.

1958
Columbia vs. Sceptre

For its part, America's Cup competition ushered in the new era with the many changes the contest had undergone in the long layoff.

The New York Yacht Club accepted a challege from England's Royal Yacht Squadron for a series in 1958. The club, after much prodding, got the New York State Supreme Court to rule in favor of eliminating the clause in the Cup charter that required the challenger " to sail on her own bottom" to the sight of the competition. That allowed a challenge boat to be fine-tuned at home and then shipped to the races where it could start fresh.

Additionally, that year, the allowable waterline length for single-masted vessels was reduced from 65 to 45 feet, opening the way for the 12-meter yacht, which remains the standard in America's Cup racing today.

During the long layoff since the 1937 race, the majestic J-class boats with their huge bodies and massive sail spreads were gone. Few could afford the large crews and costly maintenance necessary for them. The smaller hulls could move faster for several reasons, especially because sails, which continued to be triangular, had much less expanse at the base compared to the length upward. In 1903, *Reliance* had 16,159 square feet of sail, more than double the 7,546 square feet

Ranger had in 1937. Then *Columbia* trimmed that figure by 76 percent when it sailed into competition in 1958 with just 1,800 square feet of sail.

Finally, all the trimmings of 19th century Cup competition were thrown overboard. Because the 12-meter yacht now was about two-thirds the size of the J-boats, there was no room for the plush cabins, stores of food and champagne. Compactness, for the sake of efficiency, left just enough room for an 11-man crew and a boat's essentials.

Columbia was the first of the 12-meter defenders, and its crew consisted of amateurs rather than professionals. It took her all summer in 1958 before the selection committee chose her over the very capable and innovative yacht, *Vim*, to defend the Cup.

Columbia did defend the Cup, 4-0 over England's *Sceptre*, but more importantly, *Vim*, had given her a good run and Proved that in several ways a lesser boat can still be competitive.

For example, *Vim's* crew was the first in Cup competition to be housed together, a practice that continues today because the racing organizations, or syndicates as they are now known, believe it helps the members to become a homogenized unit that works better together out on the water.

1962
Weatherly vs. Gretel

Weatherly, designed by Philip Rhodes, had vied to be the 1958 defender and fell short, but after some modifications, including cutting off the transom and 18 inches of hull and deck planking, she was considered ready in 1962.

The selection committee chose *Weatherly* to meet *Gretel*, an Australian yacht designed by Alan Payne and owned by the late media magnate Sir Frank Packer. The twelve was named after Packer's wife.

The Coast Guard had its hands full with a spectator fleet of more than 2,000 boats, full of people who could just as easily have viewed the races on television but preferred an up-close look. There was so much confusion the race was delayed an hour.

Gretel, skippered by Bus Mosbacher, was granted permission to use American-made sails for the series, despite the clause in the Deed of Gift requiring contestants to use materials from their own nations. There was no sail-making industry in Australia that could produce 12-meter sails and therefore the rule was waived. The New York Yacht Club also permitted Payne, a Sydney naval architect, to use its testing tank at the Stevens Institute. The final result was a very competitive yacht, especially in medium to heavy weather.

Weatherly won in the end 4-1, but she couldn't tack with *Gretel*. That was due to *Gretel's* linked coffee-grinder winches, enabling four crew members, compared to *Weatherly's* two, to crank the Genoa sheet drum.

Gretel served notice that Australia could be competitive in the Holy Grail of yacht racing and was a force to be reckoned with in the future. This was the first of seven Australian challenges for the America's Cup.

1964
Constellation vs. Sovereign

England returned in 1964 to try for the eleventh time to win back the prize held by America for 113 years. England's entry was *Sovereign*, designed by David Boyd. She faced the New York Yacht Club-owned *Constellation*. *Soveriegn's* crew may have wished in the end that they hadn't showed up because the American boat won 4-0 by lopsided margins in each race, by 20 minutes, 24 seconds in one of them.

1967
Intrepid vs. Dame Pattie

Under strict secrecy, an important phase in mounting a Cup bid these days, the Sparkman & Stephens-designed *Intrepid* was constructed at Minneford's Yacht Yard in City Island, New York. It is no wonder such tight wraps were kept on her, for she proved to be a revolution. She had a bow with a knuckle that extended her waterline. A short keel with a small rudder attached gave plenty of lifting action and another rudder attached to the rear of the keel was primarily for steering. The combination of the two rudders made *Intrepid* particularly effective at turning quickly, which would be beneficial for the frequent circling at the start of a race. Used against each other, the rudders acted as a brake.

After a five-year layoff, the Aussies were back as challengers and would keep coming back. *Intrepid* was too much boat, however, for the Warwick Hood designed-*Dame Pattie* or any

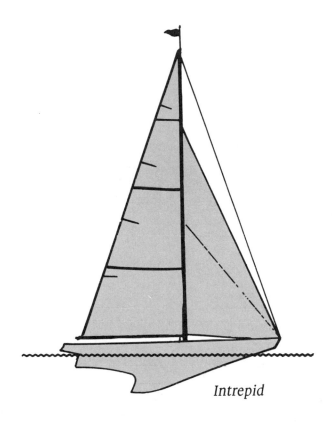

Intrepid

other boat of the period. She proved to be perhaps the most innovative 12-meter yacht ever and it is not surprising the *Dame Pattie* lost 4-0. Ironically, the next great revolution in 12-meter design would be found on an Australian boat and the Yanks would be on the sorry side.

1970
Intrepid vs. Gretel II

Some believed modifications to *Intrepid* for the 1970 race actually slowed her, but she outdid Stephens' latest creation, *Valiant*, in the trials. *Intrepid's* stern was rebuilt, she was fitted with a new keel and a new deck was put on her.

Before *Gretel II* could face the Americans, she had to get by a new entry, the French — the New York Yacht Club had agreed to allow more than one challenger, even from the same nation, run a challenge series to determine who would face the defender. Opposing Sir Frank Packer's *Gretel II* was *France I*, owned by the colorful ball-point pen inventor, Baron Marcel Bic. *Gretel II* won the right to challenge after handling *France I* easily in a 4-0 series.

Intrepid beat *Gretel II*, 4-1, but not before plenty of fireworks had been set off. The challengers were greatly miffed in the first race in which they alleged a direct hit by *Intrepid* at the start of the contest. The Americans alleged only a near-collision during the race and an international jury had to be convened. The jury sided with the Americans. Then in the second race, a regular rift opened up between the Royal Sydney Yacht Squadron and the New York Yacht Club when their yachts collided at the start. *Gretel II* crossed the finish line first but the jury later disqualified her and awarded the win to *Intrepid*. Packer did salvage some satisfaction in the whole affair by succeeding in a protest over some of *Intrepid's* fittings, which he contended were improper. *Intrepid* had to be refitted.

Intrepid later lost out in a bid for the 1974 defense but she was a popular boat and the public support for this great boat was parlayed into the establishment of tax-free donations for yachts vying for the America's Cup.

Challengers were prohibited from using American sails, equipment and assistance for the 1970 races, and following the series, the International Yacht Racing Union established rules for use of aluminum in the construction of 12-meter yachts.

1974

Courageous vs. Southern Cross

The series planned for 1973 was postponed a year as officials decided the aluminum-hull matter and various rule considerations.

Courageous was put to quite a test in the summer trials by two-time cup winner Intrepid. Under the helmsmanship of Dennis Conner, considered by many to be the best 12-meter helmsman in the world today, *Courageous* won the trials.

From Western Australia came the *Southern Cross*, owned by Alan Bond, a self-made wealthy Perth businessman who was and is somewhat outspoken. He would prove to be as tenacious as any in his desire to win the Cup.

Southern Cross earned the right to challenge by first beating the French.

During pre-start maneuverings, observers felt *Southern Cross* had fouled *Courageous*. Both sides levied protests but a jury rejected them.

While Alan Bond had had an unimpressive first bid for the Cup, the primary problem was that *Southern Cross* was no match for the likes of *Courageous*. Probably no other boat would have measured up either. The 1974 series was an important one in one respect for Bond and company: A designer by the

55

name of Bob Miller had drawn the boat's lines. Later this man changed his name to Ben Lexcen.

1977
Courageous vs. Australia

Courageous returned in 1977 but only as a trial horse for the *Independence*, or so it had been planned.

As it turned out *Courageous* proved to be the better boat in the trials, and following some modifications to adhere to recent rulings, it was she and her crew who were prepared to defend the America's Cup, not *Independence*. There was a sense in the *Courageous* camp that the crew would be a key factor in the match. The lead player in the defense was amateur Ted Turner, owner of the Atlanta Braves and TBS television network.

Turner was to face another Australian boat and crew dispatched by Bond. It was that nation's fourth straight series. In his second bid for the Cup, Bond enlisted designers Ben Lexcen and Johan Valentijn to design a vessel especially for the weather and water conditions off Newport. What they produced was *Australia*, which downed *Gretel II* and then *France I* and newcomer *Sveridge*, of Sweden, in the challenger races. Bond also had gone after the best sails possible and the best men, some of whom had been in previous Cup matchups. Despite Bond's resolute and somewhat novel approach of attacking the Cup during his second campaign, Turner and his crew and the American effort, in almost every respect, proved to be superior and easily won 4-0.

1980
Freedom vs. Australia

Skipper Dennis Conner and his crew trained a long and hard 180 days for the 1980 America's Cup races in a boat called *Freedom*, another Olin Stephens design.

Both defender and challenger in the 1980 elimination races had to give it everything to make the Cup series, an indication the America's Cup had become as competitive as ever.

Conner had to outsail Ted Turner in *Courageous* and Russell Long before he could go against the challenger.

Alan Bond was back for his third campaign with the 1977 loser, *Australia*, but some believe he was there more as a means of gleaning a few final facts for what he was already planning to be an all-out assault on the elusive Cup in 1983. *Australia* had a hard go of it with challenge hopefuls Britain with *Lionheart*, *France II* and *Sveridge* again. With a port trimmer aboard named John Bertrand, who originally had hoped to be helmsman for the series, *Australia* managed to win the second race. Bertrand noted that a 4-1 defeat at the hands of Conner and *Freedom* was due in large measure to lack of preparation. Bond, however, had at last tasted victory.

At the end of the contest, Bond vowed to return and win the Cup in 1983 and he named Bertrand to be skipper and helmsman. Money apparently was to be no object, Bond said, noting that Lexcen would design a new boat for the effort.

AMERICA'S CUP
132 YEARS OF WINNERS

YEAR	DEFENDER	NATION	CHALLENGER	NATION	MARGIN
1851	America	U.S.A.	Royal Yacht Squadron	England	1-0
1870	Magic	U.S.A.	Cambria	England	1-0
1871	Columbia Sappho	U.S.A.	Livonia	England	4-1
1876	Madeleine	U.S.A.	Countess Of Dufferin	Canada	2-0
1881	Mischief	U.S.A	Atlanta	Canada	2-0
1885	Puritan	U.S.A	Genesta	England	2-0
1886	Mayflower	U.S.A	Galatea	England	2-0
1887	Volunteer	U.S.A	Thistle	Scotland	2-0
1893	Vigilant	U.S.A.	Valkyrie II	England	3-0
1895	Defender	U.S.A	Valkyrie III	England	3-0
1899	Columbia	U.S.A	Shamrock	England	3-0
1901	Columbia	U.S.A	Shamrock II	England	3-0
1903	Reliance	U.S.A	Shamrock III	England	3-0
1920	Resolute	U.S.A	Shamrock IV	England	3-2
1930	Enterprise	U.S.A	Shamrock V	England	4-0
1934	Rainbow	U.S.A	Endeavour	England	4-2
1937	Ranger	U.S.A	Endeavour II	England	4-0
1958	Columbia	U.S.A	Sceptre	England	4-0
1962	Weatherly	U.S.A.	Gretel	Australia	4-1
1964	Constellation	U.S.A.	Sovereign	England	4-0
1967	Intrepid	U.S.A	Dame Pattie	Australia	4-0
1970	Intrepid	U.S.A	Gretel II	Australia	4-1
1974	Courageous	U.S.A	Southern Cross	Australia	4-0
1977	Courageous	U.S.A	Australia	Australia	4-0
1980	Freedom	U.S.A	Australia	Australia	4-0
1983	Liberty	U.S.A	Australia II	Australia	3-4

Chapter III

The Cup Is Lost

1983
Liberty vs. Australia II

Australia II's performance was much too impressive for some during the challenge trials in the summer of 1983 and this prompted the New York Yacht Club to wage a campaign to have the winged thing permanently docked — and the club spent its summer accordingly.

Legitimate as its concerns may or may not have been, the club's actions were motivated in part by the fear that this could be the year the Cup was lost — *Australia II* looked that good, especially in light air.

The New York Yacht Club contested both whether *Australia II* designer Ben Lexcen was soley responsible for the design of a winged keel alleged to be on her underside — though no one had seen it to know for sure — and the legality of the keel under the measurement rules governing 12-meter yachts.

If, at the Netherlands Ship model Basin in Wageningen where Lexcen tested and perfected a model of the boat, Dutch workers had contributed to the actual design, *Australia II* would be judged illegal and barred from competing. America's Cup rules require each competing nation to enter boats designed soley by its countrymen. The New York Yacht Club didn't prove the point to the satisfaction of the International Yacht Racing Union. Nor could the club convince the powers that be that the winged keel was an outright violation of 12-meter rating rules or that at the very least it necessitated adjustments elsewhere on the boat in order to bring it into compliance with the 12-meter formula.

Comically, while thousands were contentious or approving of the keel, or impartial in the matter, their dispositions toward it were largely born of faith because it remained shrouded in secrecy and well guarded under a real shroud throughout the tempestuous racing season.

Much has been said, whispered and written about the stormy events in Newport that summer but the important facts are that in the end *Australia II*, skippered by John Bertrand, and *Liberty*, skippered by Dennis Conner, faced each other just as most had predicted they would.

From an historical perspective, the passion was unparalleled. By comparison to the 1983 contest, all of the controversies in the previous 132 years of the Cup, including the ravings of Lord Dunraven in 1895, were more on the order of polite disagreements one might overhear at tea parties.

America's Cup 1983 at the time appeared to many to be the series in which the prize could be wrested from the seemingly invincible Yankee flotilla, when the longest winning streak in sport could be shattered. Regardless of what the outcome was to be the series had already been set on a course for being remembered well into the future for all of its wild thunderings, denunciations and acrimony. *Australia II*, with the magical keel, had a fantastic run through the trials to determine which nation would challenge the Americans. Competing in the trials, which ran from June 18 to Sept. 5, were Australia's *Australia II*, *Challenge 12* and *Advance*; Canada's *Canada I*; Great Britain's *Victory '83*; France's *France III* and Italy's *Azzura*. The scoring was based on a complicated point system in which early wins and losses counted less and later wins and losses counted more. The challenger race totals were as follows:

— *Australia II*, 48 wins, six losses.

— *Victory '83*, 30 wins, 24 losses.

— *Challenge 12*, 24 wins, 16 losses.

— *Azzurra*, 25 wins, 24 losses.

— *Canada I*, 19 wins, 30 losses.

— *France III*, seven wins, 30 losses.

— *Advance*, two wins, 34 losses.

The *Australia II* contingent was presented with the Louis Vuitton Cup, which along with the Lipton Cup is awarded to the final challenger for the America's Cup.

Meanwhile, three boats over in the American camp, *Liberty*, *Defender* and two-time Cup defender *Courageous*, were in a three-way race-off before the New York Yacht Club's America's Cup Committee.

Defender toughed it out all summer against the other two, which were superior boats. She performed best in light winds of around 10 knots. The stiffer the breeze, however, the less competitive she was. Finally, the blue boat was quietly dismissed on Aug. 27 by the committee.

Either the red boat, *Liberty*, or the white boat, *Courageous*, would defend the silver cup.

Unlike *Australia II*, which breezed to the starting line of the finals, *Liberty* had to fight hard from beginning to end. Which boat would win the right to defend remained in doubt until Sept. 2, when *Liberty* had sufficiently demonstrated to the club the ability to win in a greater range of wind speed than *Courageous*.

Then it began. In a 7-knot breeze, at 11:50 a.m. Tuesday Sept. 13, the New York Yacht Club's race committee placed the six-leg course settings, which vary depending on wind direction. The best-of-seven series was about to begin.

At noon, a white boat with wings and a red boat, whose backers had spent a summer letting it be known they were wary of those wings, entered the starting arena where they would maneuver for a mandatory 10 minutes until the cannon roared. Ideally, each skipper attempts to time and position his boat so that it crosses the start line at or just before the gun and with a cover on the other boat — between it and the marker at the end of each leg.

These first maneuverings were all for naught; the race was halted two minutes before the gun because windshifts had marred the integrity of the day's designated course. A second attempt was made two hours later, but it was no good, and then it was too late because America's Cup rules require each race to begin by 2:10 p.m. The yachts would have to try again the next day and the yachting world would have an extra day to wonder whether the white boat could make the impossible happen.

Under a gray sky Wednesday, and in a hearty wind of 18 knots, *Australia II* crossed the start line at 12:10:05, three seconds ahead of *Liberty*. The race was on.

They headed up the windward first leg (into the wind) and when she rounded the mark, *Australia II* was ahead by eight seconds. The second leg is the first of two power reaches in which the wind blows across the boats under normal conditions. On this stretch she increased her lead over *Liberty* to 10 seconds.

Although *Liberty* appeared to hold back on the first reach, she was the stronger boat on the reaches. By the end of the third leg, which was the other reach on the course, she'd made up that 10 seconds and had built a 16-second margin of her own.

The American boat sailed the fourth leg, which is to windward, with confidence, and by the time she reached the fourth, or top mark, she had a 28-second lead. It was with a comfortable, but by no means commanding margin, that the red boat began the course's fifth and fastest leg, which was down-wind, or in the direction wind is headed.

Suddenly, and to the amazement of the *Liberty* crew and the large spectator fleet, out from nowhere shot the winged thing from "Down Under." A quarter-mile from the fifth or bottom mark, they were neck and neck. It was predicted *Australia II* would fair poorly down-wind, but she disabused her critics of the notion and flew with the wind to her aft, her spinnaker full and proud.

Then disaster struck. *Australia II's* Bertrand attempted to jibe to port side, behind and around *Liberty's* stern, in order to gain the inside and preferred position for rounding the next mark. The maneuver was a sudden one and a costly one. It put a tremendous strain on a steering pully. A bracket securing the pully to the hull snapped, the wind deserted the white boat's spinnaker and she floundered there, helpless.

The crew worked hastily to remedy the problem, but it was too late. The red boat beat a steady, true path to windward on the sixth and homeward leg, crossing the finish line one minute and 10 seconds in front of a greatly disappointed Australian crew.

It was 1-0 *Liberty*.

Shortly before the second race Thursday, four twelves were on the water, two giving workouts to the other two so they would be keen for the impending battle. The beaten *Challenge 12* boat with a mix of some its own crew and some of those from the vanquished *Advance* worked with *Australia II*, got her to run, to spin on a dime. *Freedom* worked with *Liberty*, testing her sails, trying tacks and jibes with her, coaxing her to reach for each and every yard of water.

With six minutes remaining in start maneuvers, *Australia II* suffered another equipment failure. It was insanity. This time an upper bolt connecting the mainsail headboard to the top of the mast had broken. The mainsail, now held only by a lower bolt, had dropped an incredible 18 inches. The boat might sail just far enough to give the Aussies the valuable minutes they needed to send someone up the mast to repair it, but it might not. Bertrand first tried to sucker *Liberty* into a scheme of fouling *Australia II* and being disqualified, and he knew his opponent would consider precisely the same tactic in similar circumstances. *Liberty* didn't bite so the Australian crew instead made due, hoping they could just start the race and make it around the first mark because until they headed into the wind it would be too dangerous to send a man up the mast. Get to the first reach, then the mainsail could be repaired.

To the amazement of its own sailors, the crew of the red boat and everyone else who detected her critical situation, *Australia II*, defying her crippled condition, rounded the first mark 45 seconds ahead of *Liberty*. It didn't make sense.

Then, as if the normal way of things had somehow reversed itself, *Australia II*, despite getting her sail in order on the reach, now watched a suddenly different *Liberty* gain ground as if she had wings of her own. She didn't because her designers hadn't seriously considered putting wings on her keel. Nevertheless, the red boat rounded the wing mark, the point between the two reaches, and began to gallop. *Liberty* went on to win the race by one minute and 33 seconds, taking a 2-0 lead in the series. *Australia II*, despite having some brillant strides in her repertoir, was fast beginning to look like she would make Australia a seven-time Cup loser.

Friday was not a race day, it was judgment day. *Australia II* had protested that *Liberty* had come too close to her during a tack in the previous day's race and forced her to change course. A jury said the tack was legal and the boats weren't too close.

Also, both crews had signaled for a lay day, but the Australians protested that the Americans had given the first signal and therefore it should be assessed against their allotment. Each contestant in the America's Cup series is given a certain number of lay days, which are invaluable if it's perceived a day's weather would be unsuitable for a particular boat. It was determined that *Australia II* had signaled for the lay day one second before *Liberty*. Lay days must be called within an hour of the end of a day's race.

A starting wind of 10 knots Saturday, Sept. 17, bode ill for the third race. *Australia II* was winning going away but there just wasn't enough breeze this day. An America's Cup race must be completed within five hours and 15 minutes. It became clear early this would be a race against the clock. At 5:25, with the wind down to a depressing 7 knots, the gun sounded signaling that the time limit had expired. Light-air horse that she was, even *Australia II* found it difficult to muster more than a brisk canter while the red boat lagged far back at a mere lope.

The "little white pointer," as she was known, was having an awful time chalking up a win.

It must have been preordained that the next race, whenever it was held, was *Australia II's*, because the boat from Down Under immediately picked up where she had left off the day before. When the race was over she had ghosted across the finish line a whopping three minutes, 14 seconds to the good of *Liberty*. She stunned all of her observers into silence but Conner discussed the matter with reporters. He was asked the question the Americans least wanted to hear: Did he fear the Cup would be lost? "Well, I'm certainly aware that is a possibility," he responded, "but I don't believe in dwelling on the negatives. We are just going to do all the work we can on the positive things we have control over and hope things get better."

Monday was a lay day, called by *Liberty* following its poor showing Sunday. The Americans needed to regroup.

Liberty out-started *Australia II* at the gun for the fourth race Tuesday, Sept. 19, something it had been doing consistently throughout the series. Conner opened up an 11-second advantage and he exhibited superior sailing ability through the race, enabling the Americans to all but uncork the bubbly. *Liberty* won by 43 seconds. The tote board read: *Liberty*, 3; *Australia II*, 1. Some in the American camp — not the crew of *Liberty* — did uncork a bottle or two.

Faced with a 12,000-mile journey home if they should lose another race, the crew of *Australia II* set out with only victory in mind. There were some in the Aussie camp, especially Lexcen, who had been confident *Australia II* would perform better than she had, though they all knew that a few ill-timed mishaps had been handing her perhaps an undeserved fate. This is not to suggest that the Australians had thrown in the towel. Like many teams in sport faced with sudden death, this one could afford to come out loose with a nothing-to-lose attitude.

What the Australians got for race five on Wednesday was what appeared at first to be virtually a win by default when a port-side jumper strut on *Liberty* broke, diminishing some of the support it provides the top of the mast and thus causing the sail to sag. Perhaps the comedy of errors had selected a new subject. This occurred less than an hour before the start of the race, but by the time the gun sounded, the rig had been fixed, or so it appeared. *Liberty* apparently would race unhindered.

Bertrand had mis-timed his time-on-distance start and went over the line one second before the gun. At least in this type of racing you get a second chance, but it means having to turn the boat around, going all the way back over the line, then crossing it once again.

As it turned out the error didn't matter because *Liberty's* repair job was short-live. The jumper strut broke again and *Australia II* went on to win by one minute, 47 seconds.

The win was history. She might be down 3-2, but people everywhere were talking about the white boat. That's because for only the third time a challenger had won two races in the America's Cup. *Endeavour* had been the last to do it — in 1934 against *Rainbow*. The inimitable Sir Thomas Lipton also had done it with *Shamrock IV* in 1920.

The Aussie crew's spirits were greatly lifted for the sixth race Thursday, Sept 22. *Liberty* took a seven-second lead but that soon changed as *Australia II* turned at just the right moment into a windshift and sailed away from *Liberty*, rounding the first mark ahead by two minutes, 29 seconds.

That was the race. It was over. Just like that the boat with wings and a crew with unrivaled tenacity in the face of certain defeat made even bigger Cup history when together they sailed over the end line three minutes and 25 seconds ahead of *Liberty* and her disbelieving crew. No challenging boat in the America's Cup had ever won three races, not just in the modern era, but in the entire 132 years of the contest. More importantly for the Aussies, this was the first time a challenger had ever tied an America's Cup match. They were honest-to-goodness contenders.

What had been a pretty wild summer already, suddenly turned to hysteria — the joyous variety in the Australian camp, the oh-my-God type in the American camp. It wasn't Bertrand or any of the other 10 men who had worked the white boat into contention that found this hard to believe. They were believers. Everyone else was jerked into reality, and when they realized what was happening, they looked at one another as if to say, "Hey, these guys are good." They were in awe of *Australia II* and many now believed something in her design may have started a revolution, that she was on the verge of something great.

Friday was a lay day, called by the Australians. The "race of the century," as Conner had dubbed it, was to be held Saturday but there wasn't enough of a breeze to get a burgee dancing so there was no race that day.

Sunday was a lay day, requested by the Americans.

Light air delayed the start of the historic tie-breaker until 1:05 Monday, Sept. 26. The wind was 7 knots when *Liberty* crossed the start line eight seconds after the gun and out in front of *Australia II*.

The sails of the red boat, however, weren't catching what little breeze there was like the white boat, and when *Australia*

II initiated the first tack of the day, she came out on top. But Conner's skill won the first-leg duel and *Liberty* rounded the mark 29 seconds faster than *Australia II*. The red boat improved on that on the reach, hitting the wing mark 45 seconds in front.

It didn't look good for *Australia II*, but light winds of about 8 knots aided her in cutting *Liberty's* lead to 23 seconds at the third mark. Then the white boat faltered again on the windward fourth leg and now trailed by 57 seconds. With just two legs to go that was lot of distance to make up, but she began catching the wind at this point and might still have a chance. To have come so far and then lose would have been a blow not only to the Australians but to the entire international contigent which had fought for so long to give the Cup a new nationality.

To leeward on the fifth leg, the sailing ship with the revolutionary keel suddenly sprang to life as a freshening of the breeze injected new spirit into her watery wings. It was there, at that precise moment, in that well of water off the coast of America, that history changed its course, a course that had been good and true for these 132 years. From that point on in the race, *Australia II* and her crew simply outsailed *Liberty* and her crew. The white boat rounded the leeward mark 21 seconds in front. That meant in just one leg she had done one minute and 18 seconds better than the defender. All that *Australia II* had to do was maintain an even pace as she beat to weather on the final leg. Then she could claim one of the greatest victories at sea and in sport.

Unable to stay with *Australia II*, Conner initiated a fierce tacking duel — back and forth, first left, then right — but with each and every one of those unprecedented 47 tacks tried and 47 tacks failed it became apparent the Cup would have to be removed from its pedestal at the New York Yacht Club and be made ready for a triumphant 12,000-mile journey to a new home on the far side of the world.

The longest winning streak in international sport had come to an end. The final margin of victory was 41 seconds, but well before the end, *Liberty's* crew, members of the New York Yacht Club and stunned Americans, many of them teary-eyed, already had forced themselves to admit, "The Cup is lost."

Simultaneously, in a land of kangaroos, wombats and good sailors, millions of sleepy-eyed but devout Australians were hootin' and hollerin' in front of their teles about the time the New York Yacht Club had expected them to be in a Down-Under slumber.

Indeed, the Cup was lost, and the Auld Mug has rested these three years past in a place called Perth. Its presence there has caused Australians across the continent to brim with pride over their triumph.

Then a host of Cup-seekers from the land that lost it, and many others in the world who desired it, went to the land that won it. All were equipped with winged keels and other unknown commodities to participate once again in the greatest race under sail.

Chapter IV

The 12-meter Yacht and Crew

_____

The 12-meter Yacht

The 12-meter yacht has been the America's Cup yacht since the 1958 series between *Columbia* and *Septre*, but more than that it is the life's love of the designers, sailors and sailboat bosses who participate in this great race.

The world was not ready to renew the America's Cup challenge for a decade after the tumultuous years of world war, until a new era had been ushered in and until 18 long years had passed since the last challenge in 1937.

In 1955 the New York Yacht Club let it be known the Auld Mug was still an international prize for the taking and sought to spark the interest of the English. Who else?

Club officials asked the originators of the silver ewer whether they would be interested in a challenge if: boats smaller than those pre-war leviathans were used; and if the requirement that challengers sail their boats on their own bottoms to the defender's country were dropped?

Indeed they would, the English replied.

On Dec. 17, 1956, the New York State Supreme Court approved the two changes. In the case of the boat size, the change stipulated: "The competing yachts or vessels, if of one mast, shall be not less than forty-four feet nor more than ninety feet on the load water line." The minimum boatlength before the change was 65 feet.

The rule changes having been accomplished, the two countries agreed to use 12-meter yachts. They had been in use and raced since before World War II and had proved to be a popular class in racing vessels.

The 12-meter measurement rule, which has been around since 1920, doesn't refer solely to the overall length of the boat, but rather to a combination of factors.

The 12-meter formula is something for designers, builders and official measurers to concern themselves with, but for trivia and technical buffs the following applies: The length of the hull at 180 millimeters above the water line is added to two times the difference between the skin girth and the chain girth at the 55-percent girth situation on both sides of the yacht. Those figures are then added to the square root of the sail area. The freeboard, which is the height of the hull above the water line, is subtracted and the figure is divided by the mathematical constant of 2.37. The number resulting from all that must equal 12 meters. If it does the boat is rated as a twelve.

Although there can be no tampering with the 12-meter part of the formula, there is some latitude in the rest of it. Designers constantly experiment with variations of hull length, sail area, mast height draft and other aspects of boats. When a change in one area is made, there must be adjustments elsewhere. Thus many twelves or sailboats in other classes have more than one certificate of rating they may sail under. One certificate might be used for one type of weather, race or water, while another might be used when those conditions are different.

A very important item governing a boat's success is its

ballast, the weight it carries.

"The 12-meter rule does not tax stability," notes Bill Langan, head of the America II syndicate's design-tech team and chief designer with Sparkman & Stephens, one of the world's premier boat-design firms.

"This means that every ounce that can be saved in the hull or rig translates directly into extra ballast, and therefore, more stability and speed. Stability in Newport was important, but in Perth it's going to be doubly so because of the heavier wind conditions. We're always treading a fine line though between light enough and strong enough," Langan said.

One of the early demonstrations of the racing capabilities of twelves was *Vim*, a Sparkman & Stephens design. *Vim* drew considerable attention in 1939 when she sailed to England and raced a bit.

Two twelves stand out among all the rest. *Intrepid* and *Australia II* were "revolutionary" twelves and all the others in between and since (barring any 1987 surprises) have been what yachtsmen and designers consider to be "evolutionary."

Intrepid, which romped in 1967 against Australia's *Dame Pattie*, was the first great 12-meter. They called the Olin Stephens design a superboat. It had several innovations, including a smaller keel and rudder used for greater lifting action and a second rudder aft of the keel used mainly for steering.

The other revolutionary twelve was designer Ben Lexcen's *Australia II*, the boat with wings. Without her wings, she wasn't much different in appearance, and probably performance, than most twelves, but with them she proved to be one of the most competitive and certainly the most controversial contestants in the Cup's 132-year history. *Australia II* may have done more to focus international attention on the America's Cup than any other individual or event in Cup history. The winged keel it used is similar in appearance to the tail wing of an airplane, except that its two appendages point slightly downward. The winged keel, say the experts, gave the boat greater lift, decreased drag in comparison to conventional keels and increased stability. Although every syndicate didn't scrap all of its conventional keels after 1983, they did go into storage. Wings definitely had become the state of the art. They are being used by every syndicate and all of the twelves in the 1986-87 America's Cup trials and finals had some form winged keel on their undersides.

The 12-meter boat, which is much longer than 12 meters, is by every measure a racing machine, from its sleek and narrow hull, to its compact deck, to its computer-based navigation system. The speed of a twelve is impressive, not when compared to other motive forces — there is no comparison to planes and fast cars — but when other factors are considered; like the millions of tons of unwilling water, which it can knife through with unlikely ease; its dual nature of working with the wind and the sea when they're cooperative and defying them when they're not; and its responsiveness when driven to the outer limits of strain and stress by 11 sailors.

Despite the hundreds of millions of dollars that have been spent on 12-meter yachts in recent America's Cup races, the capabilities of the finished products have not been that great, said physicist Heiner Meldner, project manager for the St. Francis Yacht Club's Golden Gate Challenge in San Francisco.

The difference between the best twelve and the worst twelve thus far has been only 1 percent, Meldner said. Despite their similar capability when they're out on the water it's that 1 percent that can mean the difference between winning and losing, he noted, adding that the edge can be acquired through better technology.

"The top 11-man crews are so closely competitive in skills that the game today is in the technology department. It's the improvement in equipment — the boat, the sails, structural features like keels, or esoteric factors like drag reduction — that make the difference between winning and losing," Meldner explained.

Chris Dickson, skipper of New Zealand's Kiwi with the BNZ Challenge, agreed with Meldner that the differences among 12-meter boats aren't great.

"In the end all this evaluating and testing may only make a meter or two difference between us and our rivals, but in 12-meter racing that's all one needs," Dickson said.

Golden Gate Challenge's sophisticated design team, while focused on the 1987 series, also had an eye to the future of 12-meter design.

"We want to jump years ahead and come up with a computer simulation that will advance the current state of the art of yacht design by many years. We want to win. We have technological advantages over the other challengers, like supercomputers, the computer programs that go with them, and the people who know how to use this combination successfully," said Meldner, who is also president of Cordtran Corp., which has done large-scale computer simulations of the hulls, appendages and sails used for America's Cup 12-meter boats since 1973.

USA skipper Tom Blackaller, of Golden Gate Challenge, thinks his syndicate has succeeded in what it set out to do.

"Most of the other yachting syndicates are essentially giving their old boats a face lift. What we're doing is creating the fastest America's Cup racer in sailing history . . . from concept through construction . . . and frankly we're going to blow everyone out of the water," Blackaller predicted.

Tens of millions of dollars will have been spent in design and construction of twelves by race time, all the latest technology will be in their hulls, keels and sails, and countless hours of running scaled-down models through tank tests will have been spent, but knowing the course to be raced right from the start is a key to getting the most from all of the effort that goes into mounting a Cup challenge, said Langan.

Doing that means having, or in this case, building a boat principally for testing purposes, which is what *US-42* was as much as anything else.

"The most important part of our design program was sailing *US-42* in Perth last winter. There is no substitute for sailing a 12-meter in the actual race location for generating good, solid design data," Langan said.

"We spent a great deal of time trying to answer the basic length-displacement-sail area trade-off questions. This trade-off had been decided through trial and error in Newport over a number of years. We knew we would have to go through the same kind of process for the heavier wind conditions in Perth in a much shorter period. Therefore, having a boat that could do that for us quickly provided the basic input we needed. This is, of course, complicated by the fact that we were trying different keel configurations at the same time, each of which has its own optimum displacement trade-off.

"While *US-42* was sailing in Perth, we were busy trying to combine all of our research and design work with the sailing data to design our new boat, *US-44*. Because the lead time was short for the new boat, we needed accurate information on *US-42's* performance, which we got back in three ways. First, there was instrumentation and sailing performance against *Azzurra*. Second, there was America II skipper John Kolius' input. John is very good at figuring out in a very short period of time whether a boat is good or bad and accurately relaying the information we need. Third, there was (designer) Olin Stephen's input. Olin was in Perth for the (*US-42-Azzurra*) series, and I can't overemphasize the importance of his input. He knows more about 12-meter design and sailing than anyone."

The Crew

A great twelve with the best equipment money can buy will only win the America's Cup if, from bow to stern, there are 11 sailors with the talent and will to guide the vessel across the finish line first.

It is a pressure-packed contest if ever there was one, and the crew must be a sturdy sort, each a master at his own post but capable of performing any task on board in an emergency — there seem to be an abundance of those every time out.

What is pressure America's Cup style? It's guiding a twelve in a stiff 20-knot breeze with the sea thrashing about you and at you. It's hoisting, lowering or bagging sails until your arms and legs turn to rubber. It's tacking too late and then agonizing as the sails go limp, or it's failing to cover your opponent. It's trying to maintain your balance as the boat beneath you pitches and rolls and tries to toss you about in what surely must be a well orchestrated effort by the sea and all the accompanying elements that have suddenly converged right where your boat is to get you overboard and into the icy water. It's knowing that this is match racing, your boat against their boat, and despite your will to win, lurking in the back of your mind is that famous lament of losers from long ago — "There is no second." Eagle Challenge Skipper Rod Davis says match racing America's Cup style is all about pressure.

"A good match racer thrives on pressure . . . I like the pressure. And my crew and I seem to perform better under a lot of pressure. I think that's because we have so much confidence in each other. We are a very tight knit group," Davis said.

The Cup means a lot, he explained, but it's not everything. "Our crew has a little different view on winning and losing and it has nothing to do with what the scoreboard says. After the race is over, we want to be able to step off the boat and feel that we did all we could, that we did our job well. To us, that's a win."

Many of those who compete for the Cup recall having a desire to do so early in life. Davis is among them.

"Ever since I was a kid sailing with my father and getting seasick all the time, I have always dreamed of sailing in the America's Cup. Now that the Cup is out of our hands, there will be no greater honor for an American sailor than to bring it back."

The members of an America's Cup crew are likely to be among the most skilled people at their postitions in the world and highly competitive at all levels. They are veterans of any number of the biggest contests in not one but several classes of boats. They're Olympians, past participants in the World 12-Meter Fleet Racing Championships, or they might be World Youth Laser or OK Dinghy champions. In short, they've all been winners at sailing. They've spent many years, if not most or all of their lives on and around sailboats, and they've all got loads of races under their belts. They've built boats, tried designing boats, made sails and at some time or another had a taste of working every post.

To see a crew pull together, sending hands over hands, changing sails in seconds, then changing them back as fast, the skipper and navigator working every knock perfectly, the tactician calling precision manuevers and the entire operation ghosting across the line is to see magic.

To be summoned to participate in an America's Cup series is considered a great honor.

"Almost no one who has been asked to sail on a 12-meter says no," Blackaller once remarked.

The 12-Meter Crew

Bowman:

Most people finding themselves out on the bow of a twelve when there's a steady breeze would do well to get right back off.

If you don't do it for yourself, the sea will do it for you. Many an experienced bowman can tell about the time they were washed off ship.

Foremost in the bowman's mind at all times is staying on board because he knows that if a crew member is swept or falls overboard — and the bowman is the most vulnerable — too much time is expended in a rescue operation for a boat to be able to recover and get back in a race.

The bow dips below the water's surface at times, but all the while that he is hanging on to whatever is available, the bowman must at the same time perform a host of tasks. He is responsible for changing the headsails, setting the spinnaker, organizing the spinnaker pole, making certain the halyards are clear, going up the mast to make repairs, and giving important hand signals to the tactician and the skipper.

Mastman:

The mastman has a cold and wet job. What he does, he does just aft of the bow standing in a pit that is typically 2 feet deep and 4 feet by 2 1/2 feet wide. Usually, the only time the pit isn't filled with water is when the boat is sitting in the marina.

The winches controlling the halyards for raising and lowering the sails are operated by the mastman. He also attaches the spinnaker pole to the mast and assists in controlling the spinnaker. The mastman must additionally work in conjunction with the trimmers to maximize sail shape by adjusting halyard tension.

Sewerman:

It usually takes a tower of a sailor to handle this assignment, which many consider to be the toughest on the boat. Strength and good organizational skills are essential.

Part of the sewerman's time is spent on the foredeck helping with sails, but much of his time is spent below the deck in the bowel of the boat, referred to as the sewer. When he's down there — and the place is usually pretty wet — he's responsible for packing and unpacking a half-dozen or so Genoas, each weighing 80-120 pounds and a host of spinnakers. If you could look down the hatch as the bowman feeds the sails to or takes them from the sewerman you would see what appears to be a tangled nightmare in living color — spinnakers are quite colorful.

The sewerman, however, knows what's what, which is the right sail to shove up the chute.

Winch Grinders:
There are two winch grinders, one port-side, the other other starboard, and they must also be powerful men for theirs is a punishing job.

The grinders haul in the genoa and spinnaker sheets by turning the drum winches, a task only the strongest of men can perform in the time required to be competitive in match racing. When the wind is blowing against the sails and you've got to get them down in a matter of seconds, every ounce of strength must be summoned.

The Royal Thames Yacht Club was seeking a grinder and ran an advertisement soliciting interested persons. The club noted that preference would be given to "power weight lifters, rowers, wrestlers, judo exponents and rugby players."

Like the rest of the crew, grinders, of course, are subject to the back strains, pulled muscles and other physical problems resulting from their labors. They are also quite vulnerable to being washed overboard.

Trimmers:
"Trim the sails," the skipper is heard to roar at a sudden shift of wind, and the starboard and port trimmers shift into high gear, adjusting the spinnaker, headsail or genoa.

The essential physical characteristics of a sail trimmer, also known as a tailer, are long and fast moving arms to quickly handle the lines hauled in by the grinders, and a short trunk so he isn't in the way of the sails too often. If the lines aren't tailed properly, they can clutter the deck or get wound around the Genoa drum causing some serious problems. A trimmer who does his work efficiently plays an immmportant role in balancing the boat.

Mainsail or Mainsheet Hand:

If everyone else on board has done an expert job, a twelve's potential under sail won't be realized if the mainsail hand hasn't done his. His performance is critical at all times because the mainsail is the main drive of the boat.

In addition to trimming and setting his own sail and doing his own winch grinding, he must truly be a "sail master." He must continuously assess the shape of the mainsail, make certain the entire boat is properly trimmed, check the wind, and always be aware of the boat's position in relation to other boats. He remains in constant touch with the skipper, coordinating sail performance with the performance of the rest of the boat. All the while, he is susceptible to being washed overboard as demonstrated in the first race of the 1970 America's Cup finals when David Forbes, *Gretell II's* mainsheet hand, was swept over the side.

Navigator:

If Prince Henry the Navigator, a 16th century innovator in the science of navigation, could only see the computers on board today's twelves.

First, the navigator sets the direction the boat will sail for a particular race, which is dependent on several factors, including where the day's designated course is and the weather. He constantly updates the skipper on matters such as how far the next mark is and exactly how long it will take to reach it given the present wind speed and other conditions, or how far and how long before the boat reaches a favorable leg. At all times, several crew members, especially the skipper standing at his side, depend on the navigator's quick analytical mind to know precisely where they are on the 24.3-mile America's Cup course. The navigator is a tactical assistant, performance analyst and a monitor of boatspeed and windspeed. To do all this, you can bet he's got to be a veritable wizard with computers, but he must also know the strengths and weaknesses of the boat and have an in-depth knowledge of most aspects of sailing.

Tactician:

The tactician is the race strategist and he is the eyes and ears as well as the closest advisor of the skipper, who stands in front of him.

While the helmsman is steering the boat and trying to get as much speed out of it as possible he doesn't have time to know what's going on behind him, to the side or ahead. The tactician monitors everything and lets the skipper know what's happening, filtering out all but what he feels is important for him to know. If he says tack, the skipper will usually tack. If the tactician says jibe, the skipper probably will jibe.

In addition to knowing the official rules of the game — what constitutes a foul, course limits, and proper right-of-way procedures — as well as anybody and applying them during a race, the tactician is typically an experienced skipper himself and takes over the wheel now and then to give the skipper a rest.

Skipper or Helmsman:

The skipper is the director, and if the production succeeds the laurels are placed on his head, but if it fails he likewise assumes the blame.

Above all, the skipper must accurately steer the craft through every weather condition and every tactical manuever. The balance of the boat and its overall performance depend more on his handling of the helm than any other effort on board so he must be keen to this literally every second of the race.

The skipper is the ultimate decision-maker and although a good crew flows together most of the time with little backtracking, the good helmsman knows when to overrule and doesn't stand on formalities. His closest confidants are the tactician and navigator but he depends on every other crew member for input.

Boatspeed, boatspeed, boatspeed is the skipper's constant plea, on a downhill run or plodding along to wind. With that in mind, the skipper must at all times coordinate his moves with every trimming of the sails, change of sail, shift in wind direction and knock to get the maximum drive out of the boat.

Each and every skipper who takes hold of the wheel on an America's Cup yacht brings with him vast experience in scores of boats, all types of weather and water, and hundreds of races. He has at some time or another helmed boats to victory in the world's most prestigious sailing events, often previous America's Cup series.

Great sponsors, tradition, faultless organization and the most technologically advanced 12-meter yacht in the world won't win the America's Cup unless the crew, in whose hands the final outcome always will reside, is smart, strong, quick and mentally and emotionally tough. *Australia II* was a revolution, they said, and it took her seven races, and at that the margin in the seventh and deciding race was still relatively small, 45 seconds.

Here are some of the things one syndicate, America II Challenge, chose to report about the members of its crew and what is expected of each — responsibilities vary from crew to crew.

Bowman: Ron Bauman, Fred Richardson, Robbie Young.

"Robbie Young is an example of the cool, nerveless breed needed to man racing's most exposed position. The bowman is necessarily an acrobat on the narrow, often semi-submerged bow. Like a split end on a football team, he is the focal point on some of the most spectacular moments in sport — in this case, setting the huge, parachutelike sail known as the spinnaker, which must go up the instant the boat rounds an upwind buoy. The bowman also manhandles the spinnaker pole on jibes and sets up the triangular forward sails called Genoas.

"During starting maneuvers the bowman keeps the skipper and his afterguard informed as to the proximity of the starting line and the other boat. In the heavy seas off Perth, the bowman will truly be working without a net if he or any crew member falls overboard — the boat must recover him without outside assistance before continuing. (Tenders, however, may assist by fetching out the man, shutting off its engine and awaiting the yacht's return — this because of the extraordinary rough chop at Fremantle.) If something goes wrong 90 feet up, he'll go and fix it at the risk of broken limbs and a concussion."

Mastman, sewerman: Charlie Santry, Anson Stookey.

"Charlie Santry, a 23-year-old who works below deck most

of the time, knows the heat of action during competition — the aluminum hull of a 12-meter is hot and poorly ventilated. The Greenwich, Conn., native is the only America II crew member to go below.

"Like a football center, the mastman is in on every play. Every time a sail is set or taken down during the race, the mastman must unpack or repack it in the clammy interior of the twelve, better known as the sewer. He must have tireless energy. Long arms help in shoveling wet sails down the hatch and wrestling them into a sailbag. When he has a moment between sail changes, he doubles as a grinder on the main and Genoa. With the course's extra two legs (Fremantle has eight legs compared to Newport's six) his time has been shortened drastically. There is also considerably more green water pouring down the hatch on top of him, thanks to the Indian Ocean's, choppy waves."

Pitman: Beau Leblanc, Dale Vargas.

"Stationed directly behind the mast — and responsible for the halyards, spinnaker pole gear and topping lift — the pitman is the hub of a wheel. Every sail hoist or prop requires his lighteninglike hands and excellent timing to avoid terminal tangles."

Grinders: Jeff Beneville, David Caverly, Townsend Morey, Jim Nicholas, Rives Potts.

"Frequently the recipient of a colorful nickname like 'Conan' or 'Rambo,' the grinder must be built like a weightlifter, which he often is, and yet possess quick hand and arm reflexes in order to make the primary winches, or coffee grinders, fly during a sail change.

"Jeff Benneville, 28, says he 'turns a pretty good set of

handles.' The Nyack-on-Hudson native has seen 'heavyweight' competition before. For several years he crewed on the very successful maxi yacht *Boomerang*.

" 'I've always held anybody who has ever gone through a Cup campaign in very high esteem. My involvement in the America II campaign is the high point for me, especially because this Cup is unlike any other. We've got to get it back,' Benneville said.

"Since manpower is the only legal power source on twelves, grinders must have machinelike reliability and endurance — they are the tackles of 12-meter racing. During grueling upwind legs with their multiple tacks, a grinder's heart rate may soar into the 'red zone' of 180-200 beats a minute. He must also have the agility to scamper to the foredeck during mark roundings to help with sail handling."

Tailers: Kelly Gough, Andrew Hallowell, Curt Octking, Rives Potts.

"In the heat of the fray, these are the men who handle the lines which in turn control the Genoa and spinnaker. Like basketball forwards, the tailers have wide arm spans, quick hands and an instinctive anticipation that keeps the entire sail-trimming team running smoothly. During tacks they call out boat speed, which they read from digital speedometers, to the skipper.

"New Yorker Andrew Hallowell, 23, looked at several Cup campaigns before deciding to try out for America II. The captain of the University of California at Berkeley's sailing team and a member of the rowing team, Hallowell says, 'The chance to work so intensely for one goal in such an all-consuming manner justifies for me taking the time off from school. The America II campaign is the one with the best organization, timetable and outlook.' "

Mainsheet Trimmer: Larry Leonard, Tom McLaughlin.

"The great mainsail is the responsibility of the mainsheet trimmer; his adjustments and advice in sail choices are crucial. Frequently a sailmaker (professionally), the trimmer knows the meaning of every wrinkle and flat spot in terms of boat speed. After a race, he can be found advising how to cut and resew the sails for maximum output, if not doing it himself."

Helmsman/skipper: John Kolius, back-up John Bertrand, the American.

"Steering the boat is an all-consuming skill relying on years of experience and practice, requiring the requisite 'touch' skipper, that puts the boat in the groove. John Kolius . . . has an uncanny ability to get the most out of the boat. His fierce drive in the 1983 Cup trials led to his near selection — on one-year-old *Courageous* — as defender, and served notice of his claim in 12-meter competition.

"The helmsman is a thoroughbred athlete at his position, like a grand prix race car driver. He and his tactician must function as one — 'joined at the hip' — as Kolius put it. The skipper must possess such concentration skills that he can precisely steer a 30-ton yacht around a 24.3 — mile course for up to five hours when, at times, it seems like all hell is breaking loose around him."

Tactician: John Bertrand.

"A development since the 1970s, the role of the tactician has grown to include monitoring the other boat's speed and position and devising the tactics and strategy. In this, he resembles a quarterback calling his own plays. He's a second pair of eyes for the helmsman — 'a back-seat driver' as Bertrand calls it — and calls the wind shifts that are so important to the fate of a race.

"John Bertrand has worked closely with skipper John Kolius for years. A recognized helmsman in his own right, with an Olympic silver medal among his many honors, Bertrand gives America II an added dimension and serves as back-up helmsman. The tactician, along with the navigator, also handles the running backstays and backs up the mainsail trimmer.

Navigator: Lexi Gahagan.

"His job is to know at all times how the boat is doing relative to the turning points and the opponent. He tracks wind direction, records headings, advises the helmsman on tacking angles, feeds data on boat and wind speed to the tactician, and keeps time to lay lines. Although he monitors the increasingly sophisticated computer electronics on board the twelves, he must be ready to plot a course if a short circuit should occur.

"Lexi Gahagan, of Marblehead, Mass., was bowman on the America's Cup winner, *Freedom*, in 1980. In addition to his superb navigational skills, he is perhaps America II's best all-purpose crew member, serving as back-up for all positions, especially during emergencies."

Chapter V

The World Twelves

The World 12-Meter Fleet Racing Championships off Fremantle in February proved nothing if not that the America's Cup could remain Down Under for a few more years, maybe even farther down under, in New Zealand.

The America's Cup it is not, but when people talked about or wrote about the Worlds it was to the Cup their words seemed ultimately addressed.

That's understandable since the regatta, held Feb. 7-14, was supposed to and did feature 12-meter entries from most of the racing syndicates of the challenging nations slated for the Cup series.

The primary subjects of the print and broadcast media were *Australia III* and *KZ5*. Despite not facing all of the top 12-meter talent in the world, they faced enough of it to be justified in their aspirations to greatness.

Not directly related to the racing, but of considerable importance to the syndicates, the media, spectators and the reputation of the Royal Perth Yacht Club, were how the Worlds came off in the club's hands and how Fremantle and Perth stood up through the affair. Again, it wasn't so much how all this affected the Worlds but what it suggested for the America's Cup. More than the foreigners, the countrymen of the good citizenry of Perth and Fremantle, especially some Sydneysiders, were likely to be the most scrutinizing of all. The locals, who'd heard just about enough foreign and domestic doubt, no doubt were aching for the chance to vaunt their own brands of Western sophistication and savvy, to exhibit the local traditions of friendliness and charm toward strangers, and to demonstrate the universal observance of table manners in both cities.

By most accounts, the club's race committee, agencies like the Fremantle Port Authority and the people of both cities did a splendid job on all fronts — race matters, course considerations and accommodation of syndicates and spectators.
Syndicates and their boats from the following nations raced in the 1986 Worlds.
Australia: America's Cup 1987 Defence Ltd., with 1983 Cup winner, *Australia II* and *Australia III*; 1970 Cup challenger *Gretel II* by private entry; South Australia Challenge '87 with *South Australia*.

Canada: True North with *True North*, which has since teamed up with *Canada II*, the boat now leading the Canadians' America's Cup charge.

France: Challenge KIS France with *French Kiss*; Challenge Francais with *Challenge 12*.

Italy: Consorzio *Azzurra* Sfide Italiana America's Cup with *Azzurra*; Consorzio Italiano with *Italia* and *Victory '83*, winner of the 1984 Worlds.

New Zealand: BNZ Challenge with New Zealand I — *KZ3*; New Zealand II — *KZ5*.

United States: *Courageous* with 1974 and 1977 Cup winner, *Courageous*; America II Challenge with *US-42*.

Although the worlds provided some fleet-racing brand of sport and excitement, unfortunately for Cup watchers, it failed to feature some of the yachts now vying for the Cup.

Several of the syndicates in the Cup series also failed to appear in the Worlds, but the most conspicuous by far was the organization headed by a man many believe to be the best 12-meter, if not all-around racing skipper, in the world, Dennis Conner. Often unapproachable, Conner, who ended his longtime association with the New York Yacht Club to form his own challenge via the San Diego Yacht Club, was off in Hawaii preparing for the contest closest to his heart and he had with him a veritable one-man armada. His Sail America campaign christened its fourth twelve in July, five if you include Liberty, the Cup defender he helmed to defeat in the 1983 America's Cup.

Not far behind Conner's group in their conspicuous non-presence were two American contenders whose boats weren't ready, the Eagle Challenge on the American West Coast and the Heart of America Challenge from Chicago.

Australia's *Kookaburras*, named after the country's native laughing bird, weren't laughing soon after they showed up at the Worlds and decided not to play.

Parry's decision to watch the Worlds from the sideline stemmed from a requirement that competitors had to submit measurement certificates with the Australian Yachting Federation. That information then would have been available for immediate scrutiny by all of the syndicates. *Kookaburra* officials didn't like it and felt justified in their position when other nations also were reluctant to submit the certificates. The *Kookaburra* Taskforce '87 Defence syndicate led the fight against the rule.

Practically on the eve of the races, it was decided the certificates wouldn't be released until September, but in the end "it was too late," said Malcome Bailey, Taskforce '87's executive director.

"We have embarked on a race development program that makes it impossible for us to compete," Bailey said shortly after the rule change.

"Had we known two weeks ago that our design secrets would not be put at risk we would have targeted our immediate efforts towards success in the World Twelves," he added.

The friction between the Bond and Parry groups began producing sparks when it was revealed that several days before the *Kookaburra* folks dropped out they had applied to the Australian Yachting Federation for a copy of *Australia III's* rating certificate, which had been filed prior to the rule change.

Had Parry's newest twelve, *Kookaburra III*, been ready in time the syndicate might not have dropped out of the regatta. It would have provided what was to be the lead boat for the America's Cup bid with the kind of testing you can't get when sparring against one or two of the other America's Cup entries or the yacht's stablemates, *Kookaburras I* and *II*.

Another no-show among Cup seekers was St. Francis Yacht Club's Golden Gate Challenge and skipper Tom Blackaller, who along with his crew spent most of his training time in the city by the Bay. To critics who believed the racers should spend as much time as possible practicing off Fremantle and getting acquainted with the Doctor, Blackaller responded that between the waters of San Francisco Bay and out in the open sea there, he and his crew were able to get in all the pertinent practice they needed.

Also missing for the most part was Challenge France, forced to withdraw from the Worlds because of financial difficulties, but its twelve, *Challenge 12*, participated. The Marseilles-based syndicate had been on the rocks for some time and its Cup bid was revived only at the last minute.

By the time the Worlds came round, the British Challenge was still months away from launching *Crusader II* and putting her in the hands of the highly capable skipper, Harold Cudmore. He was left instead with *Challenge 12*, chartered for his use in the regatta. He was aboard to call the moves for teammate Chris Law, who was at the helm. Members of Challenge France's crew were among the crew.

Two other noteworthy rows occurred before the racing got underway.

The Royal Perth Yacht Club initiated a random measurement of boats to make sure they were 12 meters, and one of those selected was America II's *US-42*. Reportedly, the crew didn't take kindly to the presence of press and members of the Royal Perth Yacht Club, not after the secret keel episode in 1983. Australian newspapers reported that some crew members did a little pushing, shoving and manhandling to keep *US-42's* attributes from being too closely scrutinized.

Then there's the *French Kiss*. No, not that something you do with the one you love. The boat. It wasn't the evocative nature of the name, or the act, or whatever, that concerned the Royal Perth Yacht Club, which rightfully or wrongfully was beginning to remind some of the past antics of the New York Yacht Club. The Royal Perth protested that the name violated the International Yacht Racing Union's prohibition against using commercial advertising on yachts. *French Kiss* is the race horse, especially to weather, of the Challenge KIS France syndicate. KIS, stood its ground. The fear that a wave of commercialism would ensue was a rather laughable notion if you read a newspaper or magazine or turned on network television in 1986.

The prize in the Worlds is the Chandler Hovey Memorial Trophy, which was being held by the Aga Khan because he was president of the International 12-Meter Association.

Unlike the America's Cup in which both the challenge series and the finals consist strictly of match racing — no more than two boats in a race — the Worlds are run in heats with all entries doing battle against one another at the same time.

The Worlds course, the same that was planned for the America's Cup, had eight legs. Four legs, including the final beat were windward, two were downwind and the other two were the reaches in the course triangle. Like the America's Cup, the course, which ranged in length from 24.1 to 24.4 nautical miles, was designated each day depending on the wind direction. Also like the America's Cup, there was a 10-minute pre-start period in which the yachts attempted to outmaneuver each other as well as line up for a time-on-distance start in which they cross the line at the sound of the gun or as close to it as possible.

The Fremantle Doctor, the name given to Western Australia's strong southwesterlies, can be very punishing in the summer months of January when the America's Cup challenge and defender series are at full throttle and also in February for the finals. Some of the locals go so far as to say that what most of the world considers a gale is but an afternoon breeze off the coast of Western Australia. It is true that during warm-ups in the weeks before the regatta there seemed to be an inordinate number of equipment problems. Then the actual races exacted a heavy toll. By the time it was finished, some sailors were wondering what they would have to do to keep from being washed into the drink, while syndicate officials and designers were searching in earnest for what it would take to outfit their twelves for what could be a war with the Fremantle weather if it returned to normal at Cup time. Just as quickly, they were left in a quandry as the weather lightened up, but filling the mean-weather void in the absence of normal conditions were frequent nasty wind shifts of 20 degrees or more, and short choppy waves that again played havoc on bows and those who stood upon them. The wind shift meant that helmsmen and tacticians were counted on more than ever to make correct decisions and split-second maneuvers.

Scoring for the Worlds was based on the Olympic point system as follows: The winner of each heat received 0 points; second, 3 points; third, 5.7; fourth, 8; fifth, 10; sixth 11.7; The remaining boats received points equaling their placings plus an additional six points. The best six of the seven scores for each team were counted in the final adjusted point total. A fluke last-place finish couldn't knock a team out of contention because it could be thrown out in the point tally. Two last place finishes, however, would be difficult to overcome. Finally, the team with the lowest point total won.

The races:

Heat 1 — New Zealand's brand new fiberglass *KZ5* (a third has been built since), which had been on the water less than two weeks, crossed the starting line with a lead of two or three boat lengths in a 13-knot wind. Soon after the gun sounded, the wind picked up a bit and she doubled that.

By the time the Kiwi fiberglass boat — all the other New Zealand twelves also are fiberglass — rounded the first mark she was ahead of *Australia III*, her closest rival, by one minute, 4 seconds.

Then *Australia III's* spinnaker pole broke and it took her so long to repair it that despite a good recovery it wasn't good enough to win the race.

US-42 appeared to be the only boat with a chance to catch the New Zealanders in the final legs, and on the final downhill run she drew to within 32 seconds.

KZ5 had covered her well the rest of the way and won by that same margin in a race that saw Fremantle's feared blower rather tame, having picked up a bit during the contest but finishing about as it started. *US-42* finished second, followed by *Australia II*. *Australia III* crossed the end line in fourth, and had it not been for the equipment failure in the early going she might have won the first heat.

Heat 2 — There was a bit of a blow for the second heat, and all those who had or would be spending millions building twelves that could handle 25-30 knots of wind and rough seas for the Cup, breathed a little easier.

The 20-25 knot-wind at the start, which held for a good portion of the race, appeared to favor *French Kiss* until the windward sixth leg when a clew ring for her jib broke.

US-42 passed to take the lead but only briefly, because early on the final run her spinnaker became entangled. By the time she rounded the leeward mark for the final beat to wind, she was well back in the pack.

French Kiss meanwhile had corrected the jib mishap and sailed back in front to stay. *Australia III* came in 52 seconds behind. *KZ5* took third.

Heat 3 — In mild to strong winds *Australia III* was 46 seconds better than *KZ3*, the other so-called "plastic fantastic" from New Zealand. Next was Canada's *True North*, which had some inspired moments in the Worlds and proved the Canadian challenge for the America's Cup should be taken seriously.

After the third heat *Australia III* held a slim lead over *KZ5* in overall points. The two of them were comfortably out in front of most of the other twelves. They were well out of sight of six boats. For its first, second and third place wins in the first three heats, *Australia III* had been assessed 0, 3 and 8 points for a total of 11 points. *KZ5* had received 0 points for its win in the first heat, 5.7 for the second and 10 in the third for a total of 15.7 points. *US-42* was next with 24 points and she far was from being out of this Worlds. Those for whom it appeared hopeless were *South Australia*, 51 points; *Challenge 12*, 51; *Azzurra* and *Challenge 12*, 53; Gretell II, 56; and *Victory '83*, 59.

Heat 4 — The fourth race was a time for reminiscing over the finals of the 1983 America's Cup. *Australia II*, whose wings were revolutionary then, but now were commonplace, once again showed herself to be the fairest of them all when the spit on your finger barely cools while held aloft.

You could say 6-8 knots constitute a light wind. From start to finish, it was the "little white pointer," the boat that enticed the world into the realm of America's Cup racing and in doing so broke the heart of the New York Yacht Club. She won by a hefty three minutes, 14 seconds, coming in well ahead of *US-42* and third-place finisher *KZ5*.

Heat 5 — Several boats already had paid a price for sailing the fickle and choppy waters of the Indian Ocean off Fremantle, but apparently it was time for crew members to pay their dues.

Choppy water and winds ranging from 18 to 25 knots in race five combined to sweep three bowmen overboard. The first to take a plunge was *Italia's* Lorenzo Mazza, who had been gathering in a headsail on the fourth leg. A safety boat fished out Mazza, who was only slightly wetter than he would have been had he maintained his position on board. Failure by a yacht to recover crew members washed overboard without assistance results in disqualification from the race and the maximum point assessment. The Consorzio *Italia* syndicate was awarded another 21 points and now was down to virtually no chance of finishing among the top five racers.

Next to go overboard was *KZ3* bowman Robbie Salthouse, who was hauling in a headsail that had been swept over the side by an unexpectedly large wage. Unassisted, his boat retrieved him but the effort took *KZ3* out of contention and she finished near the rear of the pack.

On the second reach of race five America II's bowman, Freddie Richardson, shimmied up the spinnaker pole to free the spinnaker. It had gotten tangled around the pole when the boat luffed while attempting to avoid *Italia*, which was trying to rescue Mazza at the time. That luff put too much wind force on America II's spinnaker and it couldn't hold up. While Richardson was up the spinnaker pole the topping lift — that's the control line for the pole — gave and he and the top of the pole came tumbling down. *US-42* failed to retrieve him on the first pass, came back around, and managed to pull him back on board the second time. By then she was well back in the race. She recovered enough to finish a respectable sixth in the pack of 14.

In a breeze more characteristic of the Doctor in summer, *Australia III* again proved she was the boat to beat in good blow. She finished first, one minute, four seconds ahead of *French Kiss*, which was slowly getting its program together and performing like the good boat everyone believed her to be, especially in heavy weather. Next to finish was *KZ5*, the most consistent thus far of the top five.

Heat 6 — No offense to her renowned sister, but *Australia III* demonstrated the kind of versatility champions are made of by sailing in light winds and crossing the finish line first. She had run a smart, tactical race and came in 39 seconds ahead of *Australia II*.

With only 22.7 points after the sixth heat, *Australia III* was unbeatable even if she ran last in the seventh race. That left the syndicate with the option of observing the seventh race from the spectator fleet, which is precisely what it did. The syndicate shrugged off criticism that it was an unsportsmanlike move by countering that any of the others would have done the same or considered it had they been in a similar position.

Despite dominating the Worlds and demonstrating an ability to sail in a range of conditions, *Australia III* wasn't necessarily to be the boat Bond would enter in the Cup. That privilege was intended for a new Lexcen design, *Australia IV*, though it was in doubt for months if the yacht would even be built. With ability such as hers, the Bond people knew *Australia III* could be brought in if the new boat wasn't performing well, but after *Australia IV* was built there was little doubt it would be the lead yacht.

In a double emergency, Bond could do worse than having the first ever non-American cup winner, not to mention a boat that appeared to have a full measure of zing left in her, heading up the "Defence." True to her design plans, however, *Australia II's* prowess is realized in the calmer waters and lighter air of a course like Newport. That is what was in Lexcen's mind when he drew her on paper. Thus, unless someone could have guaranteed the Doctor would calm down to 6-12 knots throughout the Cup trials and finals, the boat that raced with wings before all the rest wouldn't have a hope of defending. Ironically, it was her radical design that both made her and broke her. So good was *Australia II* that the rest of the 12-meter world was forced to head full throttle into the world of wings, and the result has been an intense period of supertechnology in boat design. *Australia II* was docked until further notice, but it was highly likely she would be called on to push her younger sisters and their crews to their limits.

Heat 7 — First place was taken, but there remained a four-way race for second. *Australia II* was the leader with *KZ5* less than a point behind. *US-42* was a better bet for third and *French Kiss* was a likely fourth.

Apparentlly to make certain the Cup hopefuls weren't getting too accustomed to the good Doctor's change of pace, two more sailors were licked overboard, Lorenzo Mazza again and mate, Stefano Maida.

Australia II finished sixth in what was a pretty good breeze, 18-25 knots, but *KZ5* and *US-42* both finished ahead of her.

The New Zealand boat came in third and that was enough to cinch second overall. *US-42* finished second in the heat but had to settle for a third in the series.

If she was but a preview of better things to come, as the New York Yacht Club repeatedly stated, then America II's third place finish should have been enough to worry the other Cup syndicates. As regards the Worlds, however, most of the others merely noted that they expected her to do much better. With a world-class skipper in John Kolius aboard, no syndicate would be foolish enough to discount America II's chances.

Not to forget the *Kiss*. She won the race — it was her second win — by virtue of her fine hull, and on the strength of her great skipper, Marc Pajot, and his crew.

It appeared for a while that this race belonged to *US-42*. Unfortunately, a rip in the mainsail on the final downhill run gradually lengthened on the beat to home, just enough to give *French Kiss* the opening she needed to overtake the Yanks. The win by *French Kiss* and fifth overall in the Worlds assured her of continued respect leading up to the Cup. She was much improved by Cup time.

In defense of *French Kiss* and *US-42*, and to a lesser degree several other boats, in the absence of repeated equipment failures and other mishaps, the placings probably would have been tighter and in a different order.

Meanwhile, Nova Scotia's *True North* finished the Worlds in sixth place. If *Canada II* were the faster of the two boats — the combined syndicates said she was — then the Canadian challenge was likely to be a strong one.

Well back of the top six and in order of their finishes were *KZ3*, *South Australia*, *Italia*, Azzura, *Victory '83*, *Courageous*, *Challenge 12* and *Gretel II*.

The two Italian syndicates countered their poor performances in the Worlds by building new twelves. Yacht Club Costa Smeralda turned out *Azzurra II* and *III* and Consorzion *Italia* constructed *Italia II*.

Unquestionably, the major eye-opener of the Worlds was *KZ5*, which seemed to come out of nowhere to mix it up quite nicely in state-of-the-art company. They've been sailing and competing in New Zealand for a long time and Kiwi yachtsmen knew before the regatta that the team was capable of an upset. They had dreams of executing a complete upset in the Cup series with *KZ7*, the latest fiberglass product of the BNZ Challenge. BNZ merely characterized the new boat as "radical." (Not only had they constructed competitive boats for their first try but the Kiwis had picked up on the verbal aspects of the contest as well.)

Presumably, or perhaps "reportedly" is more appropriate, since syndicate folks are great believers in the power of positive thinking, the big guns of at least a half-dozen contenders were waiting in the wings, were under construction or were still in blue lines at the running of the Worlds. If the latest line of twelves turned out to be all their makers had said they would be, the America's Cup was about to embark on a new era of international competitiveness and popularity, and there were indications that era had already begun.

The Cup had definitely entered the age of commercialism with the tens of millions being spent on advertising and fund-raising campaigns by almost all of the syndicates during the three years prior to the 1987 contest.

The Cup is also surrounded by unmasked professionalism. In order to capture it, syndicate chiefs and big-name sponsors now offer greater incentives every year to design teams, management and promotional groups and the sailors themselves. Entire cities, even countries are being asked to board the Cup bandwagon and contribute to campaign funds, which governments are granting tax-exempt status in hopes of winning the Cup and capitalizing on the estimated $1 billion to $2 billion a series generates in the host city. The smiles on the faces of residents in Fremantle, Perth, Western Australia and the Commonwealth of Australia are not entirely the result of Cup pride. After four campaigns in Newport, Alan Bond had a pretty fair assessment of the millions being spent around him, so he went all out in 1983 to shift that action Down Uder and succeeded.

One thing was certain: Bondy's grasp on the Auld Mug was a powerful one. It took five tries and a daring revolutionary concept to win it, and it appeared a daring, revolutionary concept would be required to pry it loose.

The increasing international interest of yacht clubs in winning the Cup and the general public's heightened awareness of the contest and its rich history combined to make the 1987 series the most anticipated of them all. People who knew nothing about it several years before began talking about it months before the trials. The general use of the once mysterious winged keel and some of the most sophisticated racing yachts ever — including at least two revolutionary boats, *USA* and *K25* — couldn't help but result in possibly the finest and most thrilling America's Cup ever, one that measured up to its billing as the greatest race under sail.

World 12-Meter Fleet Racing Championship Results

	HEAT1	HEAT2	HEAT3	HEAT4	HEAT5	HEAT6	HEAT7	ADJUSTED POINTS
AUSTRALIA III	8.0	3.0	0.0	11.7	0.0	0.0	21.0	22.7
NEW ZEALAND KZ5	0.0	5.7	10.0	5.7	5.7	13.0	5.7	32.8
AMERICA II	3.0	13.0	8.0	3.0	11.7	8.0	3.0	36.7
AUSTRALIA II	5.7	8.0	13.0	0.0	10.0	3.0	11.7	38.4
FRENCH KISS	16.0	0.0	11.7	13.0	3.0	11.7	0.0	39.4
TRUE NORTH I	11.7	11.7	5.7	14.0	8.0	5.7	8.0	50.8
NEW ZEALAND KZ3	15.0	15.0	3.0	15.0	17.0	16.0	21.0	81.0
SOUTH AUSTRALIA	21.0	14.0	16.0	8.0	16.0	18.0	15.0	87.0
ITALIA	10.0	10.0	14.0	16.0	21.0	21.0	16.0	87.0
AZZURRA	17.0	21.0	15.0	17.0	15.0	14.0	10.0	88.0
VICTORY '83	21.0	17.0	21.0	10.0	21.0	10.0	13.0	92.0
COURAGEOUS IV	14.0	21.0	18.0	18.0	14.0	17.0	14.0	95.0
CHALLENGE 12	18.0	16.0	17.0	19.0	13.0	15.0	21.0	98.0
GRETEL II	19.0	18.0	19.0	20.0	18.0	19.0	17.0	110.0

Courtesy
Louis Vuitton Cup Information Center

Chapter VI

The 1987 America's Cup

In 1857, when Commodore John Stevens presented the New York Yacht Club with the 100 Guineas Cup and the Deed of Gift setting out the future disposition of the prize, it is likely he anticipated that many nations would vie for it.

That didn't occur throughout most of the Cups's history. Mostly, the races have been run between the United States and England or a nation in the United Kingdom or the British Commonwealth of nations. In addition to England, nations challenging in the finals through 1983 were Canada, twice; Scotland, once; Ireland, five times by Sir Thomas Lipton; and Australia, seven times.

In recent series, other nations have taken an interest in the Cup and if the past is any measure they'll soon have a burning desire for it. In 1970, France became the first non-English-speaking nation to issue a challenge. England and Australia also issued challenges to the New York Yacht club that year. England eventually dropped out and Australia won in the challenger trials but lost in the finals. Sweden issued a challenge in 1977 along with France and Australia, which eventually went on to the finals but lost again. The British joined those three in 1980 when Australia again won the trials but was defeated in the showdown.

The America's Cup at last was becoming a truly international contest, and it was apparent the racing was far more competitive than ever. People wondered how much longer the New York Yacht Club could hold on to the Cup?

Five nations were at America's doorstep in 1983 seeking the Cup. Australia, Britain, France, Canada and newcomer Italy all wanted the right to challenge. The trials were hard-fought but Australia proved too good for those nations and, of course, eventually the United States.

Add New Zealand to the 1983 international roster and you have the seven-nation line-up for the 1986-87 challenge series. The New York Yacht Club was overwhelmed in 1983 when seven boats battled for the right to challenge. As the challenger of record, the Yacht Club Costa Smeralda had a tremendous task organizing the October 1986 challenger eliminations for the 13 syndicates that would duel in the waters between Rottnest Island and Fremantle. For three months they would battle for the right to sail against one of Australia's four clubs. There were 17 syndicates in all, and there could have been more. Some organizations showed up with two and three boats and planned to wait until the last minute to decide which to sail. Four other syndicates, one from Sweden and three from the United States dropped out early. Canada's single entry was the result of a merger between the Royal Nova Scotia Yacht Squadron, Canada's official challenging club, and the Secret Cove Yacht Club, whose boat, Canada II, was selected to do the Cup racing. Yacht Club Costa Smeralda became the challenger of record because it put in the first bid.

The 1986-87 America's Cup represents the most international series to date, but it also promised to be the most hotly contested series as well with the syndicates aware more than ever of the golden future awaiting the winner of the Cup.

How golden would the future be for the lucky Cup winner? The syndicates measured it in Olympic proportions.

— The Western Australia Tourist Commission estimated that staging the contest is worth $600 million in Australian dollars to Perth alone and $1.12 billion overall to the nation.

— The Heart of America syndicate put it at $1 billion for Chicago.

— The America II syndicate estimated $500 million.

— The Golden Gate Challenge said more like $1.2 billion in San Francisco.

— Sail America estimated a conservative $600 million for San Diego.

— Baseball commissioner Peter Uberroth, who organized the 1984 Olympics in Los Angeles and now had teamed up with the Eagle Challenge, put it at $1.8 billion for Los Angeles.

Whatever the total — and it varied depending on the city, its geography and economic conditions — it was clear the Cup had become worth much more than the sheer prestige of owning it between challenges or the 134 ounces of silver it contained.

Each of the four defense candidates and 13 challengers went into the 1987 America's Cup for high stakes. The movers and shakers from their nations, states and port cities knew it, the skippers and crews knew it, the management and design teams knew it, and the syndicate heads were making sure they didn't forget it. Most conceded their quests were as much ventures of business as they were of sport.

On the surface, most of the syndicates appeared to like their chances for winning the oldest trophy in international sport, but there were lingering doubts as opponents announced completion of so-called breakthrough boats. Naturally, anything

108

less than total commitment and a maximum of self-praise from within each organization would be frowned upon by the big sponsors — names like Cadillac and Coca Cola — and the millions of people around the world who had contributed to the campaigns.

The Syndicates

For the Defence

America's Cup 1987 Defence Ltd.

Challenge issued by: Royal Perth Yacht Club
Yachts: *Australia IV*, *Australia III*, *Australia II*

Americans spell it "d-e-f-e-n-s-e," but the America's Cup was at the Royal Perth Yacht Club in Perth, Western Australia, so this time round you had to spell it "d-e-f-e-n-c-e," like they do Down Under and like they did in England when the trophy was first offered in 1851.

Eleven miles to the south of Perth is Fremantle, where America's Cup 1987 Defence Ltd., the syndicate that did the impossible in 1983 by winning the America's Cup, mounted an impressive campaign to do battle with three other Australian syndicates for the right to conduct the 26th defence of the most sought after prize in sailing. The Bond syndicate had been the only one to ever win against the Americans and was somewhat possessive of the Cup.

If the syndicate were to defeat the other Aussie groups, the

109

battle to retain the Cup would only be half over, for stalking the waters off Fremantle was a veritable international armada of 13 syndicates from six nations, all battling for the right to challenge the Australians. Each had spent millions of dollars mounting campaigns over the previous three years.

Although there are four syndicates with defence bids Down Under, most of the yachting community around the world took it for granted America's Cup 1987 Defence Ltd. would be the defender in the end.

Apart from the *America*, the syndicate's *Australia II* had probably become the most famous Cup yacht ever, but she launched a revolution in the 12-meter world, and it left her at best equal to or slower than the new line of twelves fleet. Another boat was needed.

Winged keels weren't the future, they were the present, and in order to keep pace for the Cup, syndicate chairman Alan Bond knew he would have to build a new and faster boat. Even before *Australia III* hit the water for the first time there was talk of yet another in the Australia series, though Bond had hinted on occasion that these racers were just too expensive to build privately.

Australia III's performance in the Worlds would determine whether *Australia IV* would be built, the Bond Camp had said. Apparently her margin of victory in the regatta didn't generate enough confidence, or perhaps the failure of several key boats and skippers to run in the races left Bond too uncertain of his boat's capability. If a new boat were built, one that was a little faster than *Australia III*, it might be enough to out-sail even those that hadn't appeared in the Worlds and those still being planned.

Syndicate general manager John Longley wrote in a strategy

US-46

report, "Following the World 12-meter championships . . . a decision will be made whether to build a third 12-meter, *Australia IV*. Should this be decided upon, it is likely that this yacht will be targeted for completion as close as is possible to the start of the defender elimination trials in October 1986. This will allow designer Ben Lexcen the longest period possible to develop a completely new line of 12-meter design in time for the 1986 defender eliminations."

Yes, *Australia IV* would be built, they decided. "There's nothing exciting about it," Lexcen told Defence Downunder, the syndicate's official publication.

"It's just a natural progression from *Australia III*. But if this boat's as fast I think she'll be, she'll beat the . . . .out of everything. She'll make kooka pate out of the Parry boat and send the Americans home with their tails between their legs," he said while the boat was still under construction.

Lexcen said *Australia IV* wouldn't be as exciting as some of the others. The attitude that went into her design was one of "maintaining our program of making progressively better boats," he said, conceding that such a conservative approach could backfire. "We might be too cool and lose in the end. Maybe we're kidding ourselves. But if this boat's as fast as I think she is, she'll blow everything out of the water." They were words that echoed the sentiments and words of Golden Gate's Tom Blackaller.

Lexcen, who had indicated this was his last 12-meter campaign, said the syndicate probably would go with the new boat, but he wouldn't rule out the possiblity of *Australia III* being the flagship.

With both boats entered in the defender trials the syndicate could be confident the faster of the two would surface.

Warren Jones, the syndicate's executive director and a man who helped a great deal in designing the 1983 win, said he believed the two yachts would face each other in the defender final.

Longley was praiseworthy of Taskforce '87, the defense bid he said he feared most.

"They are highly professional and certainly very worthy competitors. They are difficult people to deal with, outwardly aggressive and somewhat abrasive. But we've always said that for us to defend the Cup successfully, we'll need stiff competition — and we'll get it from them," Longley said.

Since Sept. 26, 1983, the day they did the impossible, Bond and company had been the favorite at home and abroad in the 1987 contest and were likely to remain so unless one of the other boats actually could "blow the others out of the water" during the trials.

Skipper Colin Beashel is no slouch. That was him at the wheel in the Worlds, and in 1983 he was *Australia II's* mainsheet hand, one of the most difficult positions to fill because the person must be an all-around sailor, someone with natural instinct for sailing.

If he were able to get past *Kookaburra's* great skipper, Iain Murray, Beashel then would have to tack with the likes of Conner, Kolius, Murray, Blackaller, Melges or Cudmore among others to join the ranks of the world's elite skippers. To assist him in the effort Beashel could call on a superior tactician in Hugh Treharne, the man who called the strategy for John Bertrand in 1983.

Bond, of course, was the one who had made it all possible, something he had been doing since he migrated to Western Australia from London in 1951 as a 13-year-old boy. Bond left school the following year, apprenticed as a signwriter and by the time he was 18 had his own signwriting business. For the next three years he invested in real estate and when he turned 21 the signwriter was one of the nation's youngest millionaires. Today, Bond Corporation Holdings Ltd. is the parent company of a corporate empire which includes holdings in communications, oil and minerals, motor vehicles, financing, brewing and aviation among others.

Bond's name was quite familiar around Western Australia in 1970 in connection with his business activities but that year it also became associated with sailing, particularly as owner and skipper of the 18-meter sloop, *Appollo*. Bond enjoyed success at ocean racing and his interest in that and sailing in general led to his desire to make a bid for what was to many the height of achievement of that realm, the America's Cup.

Bond had maintained that one day the Americans would lose the Cup and he soon developed the notion that he would be the one to help them do it. Such confidence, despite what was at the time a 119-year hold on the trophy by the New York Yacht Club, had been a characteristic of his since boyhood. Considering that the first campaign he waged led him straight to the finals and that he did this four times successively over a nine-year period, it seems fair to presume he was fairly in touch with his capabilities.

Bond has been the syndicate's chairman and the team captain since 1974, the year of his first try for the Cup, when his *Southern Cross* had made such a poor showing against *Courageous*, losing 4-0. The successful businessman was new at the game, but he immediately began to learn the angles of the America's Cup. It took him two more tries to discover the answer to the riddle: How do you win the Cup from the

12-METER CREW and POSITIONS

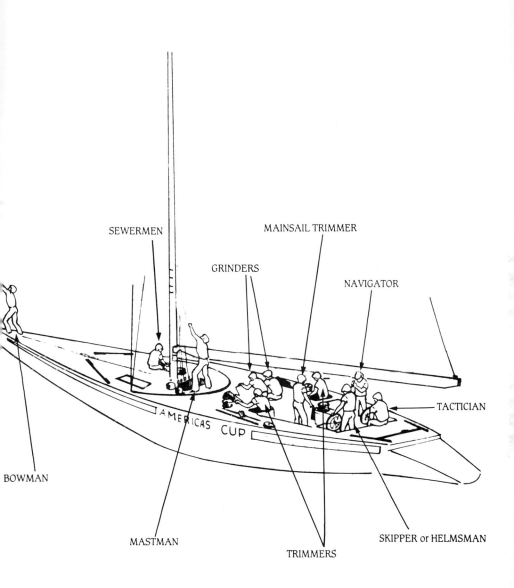

SEWERMEN

MAINSAIL TRIMMER

GRINDERS

NAVIGATOR

AMERICAS CUP

TACTICIAN

BOWMAN

MASTMAN

TRIMMERS

SKIPPER or HELMSMAN

12-METER RIGGING and EQUIPMENT

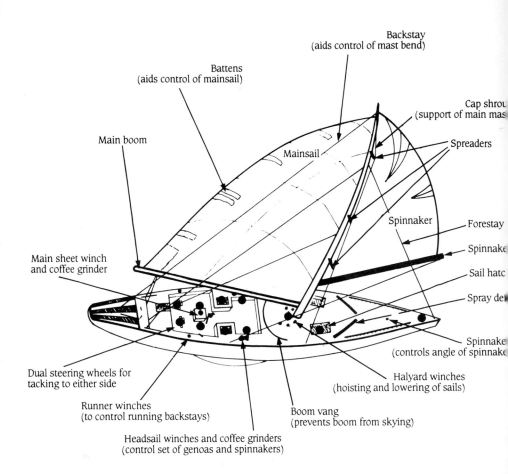

Backstay
(aids control of mast bend)

Battens
(aids control of mainsail)

Cap shrou
(support of main mas

Main boom

Spreaders

Mainsail

Spinnaker

Forestay

Main sheet winch
and coffee grinder

Spinnake

Sail hatc

Spray de

Spinnake
(controls angle of spinnake

Dual steering wheels for
tacking to either side

Halyard winches
(hoisting and lowering of sails)

Runner winches
(to control running backstays)

Boom vang
(prevents boom from skying)

Headsail winches and coffee grinders
(control set of genoas and spinnakers)

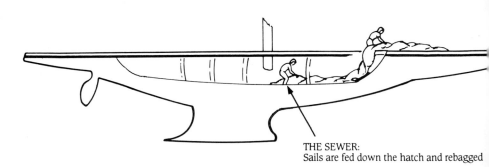

THE SEWER:
Sails are fed down the hatch and rebagged

Americans?

After the 1980 series — this was his third straight 4-0 defeat, but one which many believe he never expected to win, even before the racing began — Bond had the answer: You have to go all out. When that series was over he informed the crew and anyone who was listening, Bond and company would be back in 1983 to take the Cup to Australia. It was clear he intended to do whatever was necessary.

While Bond's syndicate also has been commonly known by the same name, America's Cup Defence is the non-profit organization which raises the funds enabling the syndicate to wage the multi-million campaigns that are now necessary to even be competitive for the Cup. Backed and chaired by Bond, the organization turns all monies over to his syndicate to be used soley for 12-meter design and construction, their tenders — the boats which accompany the racers to and from the course — crew training and other expenses directly related to retaining the Cup.

This syndicate, considered to be one of the best organized, is a large operation with a large staff. Its other two top officials are executive director Warren Jones and general manager John Longley.

Jones, whose background is in accounting and who joined Bond's empire in 1972, was manager of the 1977 and 1980 campaigns and returned as executive director in the winning 1983 effort. He and Bond became associated when Bond bought out his construction equipment and plant-hire company. The two had attended the same school, Fremantle Boys High, though they were a couple of years apart.

Longley started out as a math and science teacher with the Western Australian Education Department. He taught at the secondary level for three years then went to London to teach for a while. Longley had another interest. He was one of Australia's best yachtsmen, having started out sailing on the Swan River in Perth when he was 13. Later he went into ocean racing. Aboard the *Hotspur* at the 1968 Syndey-to-Hobart race he met Alan Bond, who was racing *Apollo*. Bond later persuaded Longley to be his foredeck boss for the Cowes Week series in 1971. A crew member for every Bond challenge, Longley continued teaching and sailing in international events until after the 1980 Cup series when Bond asked him to be project manager for the 1983 challenge. Longley, who in 1986 lived within walking distance of America's Cup Defence headquarters in Fremantle Harbour, accepted Bond's offer. In addition to his organizational duties, as a grinder for the 1986-87 series Longley continued to perform one of the toughest jobs on the boat as well.

An integral part of every good syndicate is a good designer or design team. In this case it's Ben Lexcen, without whom, arguably, Bond may not have won the Cup in 1983. Since he had indicated the 1983 series might be his last campaign if it failed, he might never have known the thrill of winning the Cup without Lexcen's revolutionary keel boat.

Lexcen is the man who drew those revolutionary, winning wings for Australian II. His work has since influenced designers all over the world and changed the face of the America's Cup, or at least the undersides of the boats that compete in it.

A native of Bogabri, New South Wales, Lexcen received no formal education until 1947 at the age of 11. Three years later he left school to do an apprenticeship as a fitter and turner with New South Wales Railways and upon completion went to work as a maintenance fitter for an aviation company.

Lexcen was interested in sailing most of his life and when he was 17 he crewed with a boat that won a Star Class championship. Apparently not cut out to be a maintenance fitter, he started his own sailmaking business in Queensland, Australia. While there, he designed and built an 18-foot skiff, which was called *Taipan*. That was in 1961. The following year, he designed and built another 18-footer, *Venom*, and it won the world championship in its class.

Now it was definite, Lexcen was not cut out to be a maintenance fitter, but he was not only a natural-born designer, he was also a pretty fair sailor. In the Flying Dutchman class he won six Australian championships. Then he went into the Soling class and represented Australia at the 1972 Olympics at Munich, West Germany.

Throughout this period he continued to design boats, 18-footers, dinghies, revolutionary boats in the Maxi class, two boats for the 1972 Admiral's Cup, six winners for the Hobart race and others.

Despite a wealth of success before his name was ever associated with the America's Cup, Lexcen undoubtedly will be remembered most of all for *Australia II* and her winged keel. Other 12-meters he has designed for America's Cup competition include: the 1974 challenger, *Southern Cross*; the 1977 and 1980 challenger, *Australia*; *Challenger 12*; and for 1987, *South Australia* for the South Australian syndicate and *Australia III* and *Australia IV* for the Bond syndicate.

After *Australia III's* first sail in late 1985, Lexcen said, "It felt like it was doing 5,000 miles an hour . . . I let the steering go for a mile and a half and she steered herself. Everything in the boat is perfect."

Then what about *Australia IV*, the boat the syndicate

hoped would keep the Cup in Perth?

Australia IV "is an ordinary boat," the designer said, but he was only referring to her appearance compared with some of the flashy twelves slated for the Cup series in Fremantle. The truth is that tank tests convinced Lexcen that *Australia IV* might just prove to be the fastest twelve in the world. Who could argue with him?

A footnote to all that has gone on in the Bond camp is the future of *Australia II*, the boat around which legend has sprung sprung in the land Down Under and the international yachting community. She is to be a national treasure, purchased for $2 million by the commonwealth in a tribute to her contribution to the nation's heritage. Like Phar Lap, the great Australian gelding, she has touched the heart of a nation and will go on permanent display in a museum someday. She has proved recently she still can fly, however, as proven in a decided victory in May over *South Australia* for what was slated to be her final race. It was highly unlikely she would come out of her Fremantle stable for a rescue operation — only the direst of emergencies could have caused that to happen. If, however, in the wildest imaginings of the most incurable romantics, the winged wonder were called upon for an heroic sail and, still more incredible to dream about, were to successfully defend her Cup, it boggles the mind to conceive what manner of reverence the people of a continent would show her, and justifiably so.

Taskforce '87 America's Cup Defence

Challenge issued by: The Royal Perth Yacht Club
Yachts: *Kookaburra III*, *Kookaburra II*, *Kookaburra I*

Is it possible for a kookaburra to box the ears of a kangaroo?

Logically speaking, no, but the funny little bird which appeared on the burgee of Taskforce '87 most definitely put the "roo," its cross-town rival that appears on the pennants of Bond boats, "up a gum tree," to use a purely Australian expression.

Under the beneficence of Perth businessman and Australian television network owner Kevin Parry, the *Kookaburra* syndicate mounted what was considered to be one of the more formidable Cups bids and, starting from scratch he had done it in a relatively short period.

Not long after *Australia II* won the Cup, Taskforce '87 was born. It started when Parry was listening to a luncheon address from a triumphant Alan Bond, who called for support to keep the trophy in Australia. Seventeen months later the first of the *Kookaburras* was launched.

With no other twelves to work with, the young syndicate faced going to the defence trials with no real gage of its boat's capability. Taskforce '87 made it known the *Kookaburras* would race against any twelve in its preparation for the defence series.

Syndicate chief executive, Malcolm Bailey, said the move was criticized by some — he didn't say by whom — but he explained Taskforce '87's position.

"Our position is quite clear. We want to trial with as many 12-meters as possible. One of the problems of racing 12-meters is that there simply aren't too many of them. It's not something we have rushed into by any stretch of the imagination. We look carefully at the benefits for our syndicate and make our decisions based on that judgment."

Bailey said the syndicate benefited in several ways by its open trial policy.

Courageous IV

122

"When you look at the psychological advantages for the crew alone, it is simply common sense. If we, and let me say that I certainly believe we will, have to race the Americans or the Italians in the America's Cup, our men will not be daunted by it. They will not be over-awed because they (will) have done it before, all as part of their training for this event," he said.

Not surprisingly, the Bond syndicate feared Parry's *Kookaburra* challenge more than any other in Australia. The reason was partly because the boats had fared well against a host of Cup contenders and partly because Parry's project director and *Kookaburra* skipper Iain Murray, was recognized in most circles as Australia's premier helmsmen.

Sailing since he was 10, Murray has built up an impressive list of credentials, one that is as long as a twelve. He was named 1985 Ampol Yachtsman of the year, Australia's most prestigious yachting award. He holds the further distinction of being a co-designer of the *Kookaburras* along with John Swarbrick and Scott Kaufman. At the America's Cup level of competition, skippers often are skilled sail makers but the skipper-designer combination is rare.

Like most of the syndicates, Taskforce '87 had to maintain many more than the 11 crew members who would eventually race in the trials. Not only are backups needed for the first crew but a capable second crew also is needed so its performance as a jousting partner is of a standard that it will truly test the mettle of the starting team.

A great deal is demanded of each crew member on an America's Cup team.

The day begins at 5:30 a.m. for a crew member of Taskforce '87 and it doesn't end until the late afternoon or early evening.

First, there is running and then a gymnasium workout, which is individualized for each crew member.

Next, they eat breakfast and like all meals it is specially prepared.

"They're on a basic cereal breakfast (and) lots of fruit . . . Basically they have a very limited amount of really fatty foods (and there is) more emphasis on the more complex carbohydrates," said Grant Donavan, a sports psychologist who, along with exercise physiologist Charles Cochrane, worked closely with the crew to ensure maximum mental and physical conditioning.

Sometime before mid-morning the crew boards their twelve. They sail and compete for six hours without a break; there's no stopping for tea or a formal lunch. Hunger is a problem, however, so fruit is carried on board.

"It's a demanding program and a lengthy one, too. It will take a special breed of sportsman to be able to handle it," Donavan said, adding that "the beauty of a 12-meter campaign is that the crew can see that ultimate goal at the end of it all.

"We place the responsibility back on the crew — if they want to be successful then they have to go out and put the time and effort in themselves. It's quite autonomous — they are all part of the decision-making process and we have had remarkably few hiccups over the past eighteen months. They're a top bunch of guys and we were lucky that many of them knew each other already, despite the fact they came from opposite sides of Australia."

While they're out sailing, crew members have electrodes strapped to their chests and wear special watches. This is done so Donavan and Cochrane can monitor the physical and mental effects of the day's work.

After the yacht is docked for the night, there is cleanup, any necessary equipment repairs and installation of new gear and a debriefing in the crew conference room.

"Some go and have another workout before they go home or if something major is happening they'll return home for dinner briefly and be back down at the dock to continue work in an hour or so," Donavan said.

The people with Taskforce '87 were well aware that while their bid for the Cup was getting some high praise, there was still an underlying feeling by most that Bond and company were the favorites.

That may have explained in part the fierce feud that existed between the two syndicates or it may have been the sheer proximity of the two groups — both are based in Perth. Trying to get the support of the same hometown folks and bumping into to each other on the doorsteps of the big sponsors without whom Cup bids would fail also may have caused the strained relationship.

Whatever the causes, as noted in chapter V, the feud heated up just before the Worlds over the 12-meter ratings certificates. Later when the public became aware of the problem a scolding was issued by the Royal Perth but matters only seemed to worsen as the defender eliminations neared. A statement by one of Parry's men contending that *Kookaburra II* had clearly emerged the best boat in a special defenders' meet initiated by the Royal Perth clearly incensed Bond's group. Reportedly, a prior agreement had been reached in which the syndicates had agreed to make no statements about the outcome of the friendly sail, which featured *Kookaburra II*, *Australia II* and III, and *South Australia*. Parry's group apparently also failed to give proper emphasis to the fact that the races were on an approximately 2-mile course and therefore absolute comparisons couldn't be made to the 24.3-mile America's Cup course. The bad feelings between the two syndicates nearly resulted in a ramming incident between their boats.

Kookaburra officials did a couple of things which are quite common in the world of the America's Cup but which may have nixed any chance of patching up the bad feelings. First, they went after British yachtsman Lawrie Smith, who they hoped to employ as a helmsman for one of the *Kookaburras* during the defender trials. Smith had to be judged an Australian citizen before the move could be finalized. Next and worse yet, they snatched Peter Hollis away from — you guessed it — Bond and company and planned to use him as a tactician.

Through it all, the Royal Perth's interest has been to maintain the integrity of the Cup. The club also wanted to avert a situation in which the nation's two top contenders, having become such bitter enemies, directed so much energy against each other that they failed to adequately prepare for the challengers. That seemed unlikely, however, considering the vast resources both syndicates had at their disposal due to their wealthy benefactors, Kevin Parry and Alan Bond.

South Australian Challenge for the Defence

Challenge issued by: Royal South Australian Yacht Squadron
Yachts: *South Australia*

Adelaide, the capital of South Australia, is a long way from Fremantle but the two cities both went into the defender trials with one important person in common so far as the America's Cup was concerned.

Both had boats designed by Ben Lexcen, designer of the great *Australia II*.

The Bond Camp was not likely to take the South Australians too lightly, particularly since Lexcen had indicated the boat was about as fast as *Australia II*. The 12-meter rule is flexible enough that members of a high-tech design team may can refurbish a boat into a winner, which is what the South Australians and other syndicates attempted to do.

John Bertrand, the man who skippered *Australia II* to victory in 1983, expected the South Australians to come on strong about the time of the defender trials. He also recommended they get John Savage, who had been with the Bond campaign as an alternate skipper. Savage, who also skippered *Challenge 12* in 1983, indeed was acquired by the South Australians to be a co-helmsman with young Phil Thompson, of Sydney. The two of them were expected to provide the group with solid helmsmanship. It took some time before the syndicate felt it had just the right skipper. Sailing director Sir James Hardy gave the wheel over to skipper Fred Neill at the Worlds, then it was thought the nod would go directly to Thompson, but instead Savage turned up.

After finishing eighth in the Worlds, *South Australia* underwent considerable physical changes, including to her keel and the sail arrangement, and she supposedly came out quite faster than before. Nevertheless the experts weren't picking her to upset her countrymen in Western Australia.

Like the Eastern Australian syndicate in the neighboring state of New South Wales, South Australia's major problem throughout was raising the funds for waging a legitimate campaign.

In 1985 the South Australian government, aware that the

Crusader I, Crusader II

syndicate in its state was faltering without funding, stepped in to help.

"When the government decided to get behind the challenge we did so because we believed that *South Australia* had had a bit of a rough time," South Australian Premier John Bannon had said.

"We were in danger of getting a reputation as the 'Cinderella State.' We needed a few projects with flair and imagination — projects which were bold and exciting. We needed some things happening in this state to show the rest of Australia and the world that we were here, that we were ready and capable of mixing it with the best," Bannon said. The South Australians had to scratch for the big sponsors, the ones that could give six-figure sums to the campaign, and syndicate chairman Graham G. Spurling had to do so at a time when a lot of those sponsors had been grabbed up by the two western syndicates, which were known to have the kind of organizations, boats and crews to be viable in the contest.

Eastern Australia's America's Cup Defence

Challenge issued by: Royal Sydney Yacht Squadron
Yachts: *Steak 'n' Kidney*, Australia

The *Steak 'n' Kidney*

Unless you are hungry
Or live in Sydney,
You might not savor,
The *Steak 'n' Kidney*.

What brave historian
So boldy recorded,
That race of the *Steak 'n' Kidney*.

When o'er first she ghosted
Distant foes eyed her glibly.
Said her ravaged-looking skipper,
"Bloody-damn right, *Steak 'n' Kidney*."

The name caused a bit of an upheaval at first. It just didn't seem to go down well with a disbelieving crowd that had gathered before the grandiose Sydney Opera House for the naming ceremony. Then, after a while most learned to stomach it. A few Sydneysiders, their city being the obvious brunt of the name — in this case, a little tasteful humor — admitted to not minding the peculiar name, not if it could bring home the bacon.

The name is the brainchild of Powerplay, the sports marketing agency hired by the Eastern Australian syndicate to beef up the program. Powerplay's bright boys and girls came up with *Steak 'n' Kidney*. Starved for funds and name recognition, the syndicate decided something spectacular simply had to be done or the whole project would go aground. The Sun, a Sydney newspaper, had played a significant role in the Cup bid, so the name, Sunshine, was contemplated but it was decided the name just didn't arouse people's emotions enough. In addition to the *Steak 'n' Kidney's* play on Sydney to get people there to pitch in a few Australian dollars, the syndicate billed the vessel as the people's boat, hoping to appeal to the working man's appetite for being a part of something that had heretofore been reserved almost exclusively for the wealthy.

What of designer Peter Cole's beautiful long, white twelve,

his first, which one can't help but picture with food all over it? There are some who say she is not unlike many of the world's fastest twelves in physical appearance so if she were able to knife though the Indian Ocean like she appeared she could — who could say what the chances for an upset might be? The boat was built to have a strong hull with plenty of volume in the ends in order to give her the toughness needed to cope in the waters off Fremantle. A high freeboard also was designed to help in that regard. Cole also gave *Steak 'n' Kidney* lines meant to provide her with good acceleration out of a tack.

Olympic Soling veteran Gary Sheard, of Melbourne, did the initial sailing of the new boat and was named as lead skipper. Skipper Graham Jones, who had had considerable match-racing and 6-meter experience, also was acquired in mid-1986. The twelve's trial horse was 1977 and 1980 Cup challenger *Australia*, which the syndicate acquired from the British.

The Eastern Australian group organized primarily because well-known businessman and off-shore racer Syd Fischer, and others on the east side of the country decided they wanted to be in on the America's Cup, the defense if possible. Several groups had been going it alone and weren't able to muster adequate campaigns, so they all got together. Moreover, the rivalry that often exists between east and west coasts is quite prevalent in Australia, so the opportunity to compete against those hot-shot sailors over in Perth appealed to a lot of Syndeysiders.

"It's important the people of Eastern Australia feel part of this historic effort," syndicate fundraising chairman Peter Hadfield said, adding, "There seems to be an idea that the only ones with a chance of defending the America's cup live on the other side of the continent."

Unlike the Bond and Parry powerhouses, Fischer's syndicate rationed every dollar, withholding any funds that might have gone for appearance's sake rather than for absolutely vital equipment and preparation.

"The syndicate has developed a no-frills approach to the America's Cup Defence. No money will be lavished on unnecessary extravaganzas. All funds are ear-marked for one purpose only, to make (the *Steak 'n' Kidney*) achieve her maximum performance.

Despite the kind of grass roots and amateur spirit that marked the campaign, and having a boat with a little something extra on it, the *Steak 'n' Kidney* bid may have been a bit of a short order for this series. While amateur might not be quite the proper term — Fischer was trying to do the job for far less than the going campaign cost of $20 million — expenditures were well under those of most other syndicates. The comparatively low budget resulted in numerous financial and organizational problems as Fischer's group tried to gear up to America's Cup speed. A broken mast that took the wind out of their sails for a couple of weeks didn't aid matters. Only the likes of a sailor such as Capt. James Cook, the first European to set foot in the Botany Bay area near Sydney, may have been capable of staging the kind of an upset required to outdo the boys from Perth or even neighboring South Australia.

Syndicate fundraising chairman Peter Hadfield wasn't too concerned over the late campaign.

"Winning in any sport is all about reaching your peak on the day, and our late entry into the Australian selection trials with this fine yacht and our careful program of crew training is designed to achieve just that," Hadfield said.

The Challengers

Sail America Foundation for International Understanding

Challenge issued by: San Diego Yacht Club
Yachts: *Stars & Stripes '87*, *Stars & Stripes '86*, *Stars & Stripes '85*, *Liberty*, *Stars & Stripes '83*

While the America II Challenge was being labeled as one of the most feared syndicates by the Aussies, there is little doubt Dennis Conner was the skipper who worried them and just about everyone else the most.

Conner maintains a large following of professionals and fans who believe him to be the best 12-meter sailor in the world, and that despite steering *Liberty* to defeat and losing the Cup in 1983. The Australians see in him a man who does not like losing. After 1983 Conner set out on a rigorous, somewhat reclusive physical and mental campaign, not only to win the Cup back but possibly to atone for having been at the helm when it was lost. There is widespread agreement the Cup was ripe for the taking in in 1983 because there was an arena of unprecedented competitiveness.

Here's what some of the major publications in the world of sailing and elsewhere had to say about Conner for 1987.

"More than any other individual he's still cited as the man to beat," wrote Motor Boating & Sailing magazine.

"Dennis Conner's San Diego Yacht Club-based syndicate is rated most likely to succeed . . . in the eyes of top players in Alan Bond's *Australia III* defense syndicate," said Sail magazine, prior to the construction of *Australia IV*.

"Conner is the man to beat," wrote the Washington Post.

"Dennis Conner is the favorite to win the right to challenge," wrote Yacht Racing/Cruising magazine.

Despite the wealth of comment about him — it's not all complimentary — Conner said virtually nothing about any of it while training in Hawaii from September 1985 to August 1986, apparently preferring instead to allow his and his crew's performances to serve as his voice. If he says anything, it's usually not in public and if it is, it's fairly certain the media won't be present. After the racing, he's like most people, more willing to discuss it if he was successful, reluctant if he was not. He spoke to the media fairly regularly in 1983.

The closest most reporters come to quoting Conner is by quoting someone willing to speak about him or someone who has permission to speak on his behalf. With such elusive and notable public figures, reporters always are anxious to get something, two or three words, anything. There was little to get during his seclusion. One of the most widely used direct quotes from Conner came from a Western Australian television advertisement in which Conner appeared on behalf of the state lottery and said in part, "Hi, remember me? I'm the guy who lost the America's Cup." He hadn't lost his sense of humor. Reporters were able to get a direct quote, albeit via television, and the novelty of the commercial was enough for them to weave entire stories around it. Still, as the *Stars & Stripes* campaign gradually came together Conner did show signs of accepting the inevitable role of being a media attraction. Apparently, he had merely been busy getting down to business, but when it came time he was prepared to re-emerge.

Sail America cornered the market for the most talent at the helm by coming up with the tandem of Conner and former *Courageous* skipper Peter Isler, whose ability to guide a twelve

Race Predictions Committee Syndicate Ratings

	Adminis-tration	Hull/Keel	Sails	Skipper/Tactician	Crew	Computer Analysis & Tuning Facilities	Moti-vation	Entre-preneurial Business Acumen	TOTAL	June Update
AUSTRALIA										
Australia III Perth	9.0	8.8	9.0	8.6	8.6	8.8	9.0	9.0	70.8	72.0
Kookaburra Perth	6.8	7.8	8.2	8.0	8.4	8.8	9.0	7.8	64.8	65.4
South Australia Adelaide	6.2	8.2	6.2	4.4	5.2	6.2	6.6	4.6	47.6	47.8
Eastern Australia Sydney	3.8	5.6	4.6	4.6	4.6	3.6	5.0	4.8	36.6	37.0
U.S.A.										
Stars and Stripes San Diego	8.8	8.8	8.8	9.0	8.4	9.0	8.8	8.8	70.4	71.8
America II New York	7.6	8.4	8.8	8.2	8.0	8.4	8.6	8.8	66.8	68.2
USA San Francisco	8.0	8.0	7.0	9.0	7.0	8.0	8.0	8.0	63.0	62.2
Eagle Newport Harbor	7.0	8.2	7.6	8.8	7.8	7.0	8.6	6.6	61.6	62.4
Heart of America Chicago	4.6	5.8	6.8	8.2	7.0	5.0	7.4	5.2	50.0	50.8
Courageous New York	4.6	5.6	6.4	5.0	5.8	7.2	6.8	7.4	48.8	48.0
ITALY										
Azzurra Costa Smeralda	7.6	7.0	7.4	5.4	5.8	6.6	5.4	8.0	53.2	53.2
Italia Genoa	6.6	6.8	7.6	6.0	6.0	6.8	6.0	6.8	52.6	52.6
FRANCE										
French Kiss La Rochelle	7.8	8.4	7.4	6.8	6.4	6.6	6.4	7.8	57.6	55.6
Challenge France Marseille	4.2	5.0	5.0	4.0	4.0	4.8	5.0	3.4	35.4	35.2
BRITAIN										
Crusader London	5.6	7.8	6.6	8.0	7.6	6.2	8.0	5.8	55.6	56.6
CANADA										
Canada II British Columbia	4.8	5.8	6.8	7.4	7.6	4.2	7.6	5.0	49.2	49.2
NEW ZEALAND										
New Zealand Auckland	7.8	8.2	7.8	8.2	8.6	7.6	8.8	8.6	65.6	64.3

would easily make him a top candidate for a starting role if it weren't for the presence of the man himself. Isler lost his Corinthian spirit when it was decided the *Courageous* challenge wouldn't build a new boat as planned. He didn't want to be teamed up with what he considered to be not enough boat. The syndicate decided to touch up the old boat and give it a new name — *Courageous IV*.

Like its two predecessors, *Stars & Stripes '87*, the yacht Conner was planning to skipper in the Cup, is 65 feet long, 45 feet at the waterline, has a 90-foot mast, 1,200 feet of sail on both the Genoa and the mainsail and weighs 50,000 pounds. Nothing was disclosed about her keel, a little trick the boss learned first-hand in 1983 from the Australians. Conner left a doubt as to which boat the syndicate would sail because there had been such good results in 20-knot plus winds off Hawaii with *Stars & Stripes '85*. That kind of force is what sailors expected to have to contend with until the Doctor threw a question mark into the planning by being uncommonly passive during the Worlds; nevertheless, all of the syndicates planned for strong wind.

Meanwhile, it seemed for a time Sail America and other syndicates would keep building twelves right up to Cup time or until it was certain there would only be enough room in Fremantle Harbour for boats bearing their logos. The building did stop and by the northern summer's end the final vessels had tasted plenty of seawater.

Would Conner be a good bet to recapture the Cup? Yes, probably the best bet of all. The major question was whether he could come up with the right boat to do it. Sail America believed it had covered that base by putting together a technological all-star design team that included Charles Boppe of Grumman Aerospace, NASA scientists, Louis Gratzer with the Boeing Flight Research Institute, various technical consultants and San Diego Pentagon subcontractor Science Applications International Corporation. Stars & Stripes '87 was designed by Brit Chance, Bruce Nelson and Dave Pedrick.

Anyone who has seen Dennis Conner sail a 12-meter yacht over the years knows skippers don't come any better, so it is no wonder that the rest of the field in 1987 pointed to him as the skipper they most feared. After his defeat in the 1983 Cup series, Conner broke with the New York Yacht Club syndicate, which he'd done battle for in the successful defenses of 1977 and 1980. Following the 1983 series he went to San Diego where he has his home and business, Dennis Conner Interiors. No one doubted he would be back in 1986 to compete in the trials for selecting a challenger to go up against the Australians Jan. 31, 1987, in the Cup series.

In San Diego Conner helped establish a new syndicate, the Sail America Foundation for International Understanding, which sponsored his *Stars & Stripes* campaign. In addition to sponsoring the Cup bid, Sail America was formed to further amateur sailing competition and to promote international understanding and education through sailing as well as to promote good sportsmanship among the youth of America.

Key people with the Sail America team include Conner, foundation board president Malin Burnham and executive administrator H.P. "Sandy" Purdon, John Marshall and George F. Jewitt Jr.

Conner is a trustee of the foundation but more importantly he was the man the entire organization looked to more than anyone else to bring the Cup back to America, and more specifically, to the San Diego Yacht Club, which celebrated its

100th birthday in 1985. Conner's sailing credentials: winner of four Southern Ocean Racing Conference titles; two Congressional Cup races; two Star World championships; an Olympic bronze in 1976; skippered for two Admiral's Cup teams; tactician and helmsman in two successful defenses of the America's Cup, *Courageous* in 1974 and *Freedom* in 1980, and skipper of *Liberty* in 1983; and commodore of the San Diego Yacht Club in 1984.

Burnham's sailing credentials include many years of competition in Star class with finishes in first, second, third, fourth and twice in seventh place. He was skipper of *Enterprise* during the 1977 America's Cup defender trials and assisted as a skipper in other campaigns. He was president of the International Star Class Yacht Racing Association from 1978-83 and commodore of the San Diego Yacht Club in 1967. He holds memberships in the San Diego Yacht Club, St. Francis Yacht Club in San Francisco and the New York Yacht Club.

Purdon, like many of those who help to run the syndicates, brought considerable sailing experience. He has won more than 30 major yachting events trophies in International Ocean Racing in Southern California, long distance racing in Mexico and Transpac competition. He is a past director of the Southern California Racing Association, former fleet captain of the Ocean Racing Fleet and has chaired a number of major regattas.

Marshall, an Olympic medalist, came on board to be the *Stars & Stripes* design team coordinator and a Sail America board trustee. His sailing background included participation in four America's Cup defenses — he was mainsheet trimmer and tactician on *Freedom* in 1980 and *Liberty* in 1983.

Jewett, a close friend of Conner's for many years, served as the defense chairman in the 1977, 1980 and 1983 Cup

Stars and Stripes '87

campaigns.

Sail America's $20 million America's Cup campaign may have been the most thorough and intensive, not only among the 1987 hopefuls but perhaps in Cup history. With conditions to his liking, and barring the emergence of a twelve so superior that no amount of preparation would offset it, Conner seemed a likely candidate certainly for the final four among the challengers and quite possibly the finals. With a good boat his unrivaled start maneuvers were likely to be on display during the 10-minute prestart Jan. 31, 1987 for race one of the America's Cup.

Conner's predictions among the challengers were that his own group and those of America II, the British and New Zealand would be the four finalists.

America II Challenge

Challenge issued by: New York Yacht Club
Yachts: *US-46*, *US-44*, *US-42*

The only things the New York Yacht Club didn't do to bring about the America's Cup were to order the silver cup and then to offer it as a prize. The club was as responsible as any other entity for the start of the great contest.

Setting aside everything bad anyone has ever said about the club, without it the America's Cup race would not exist, not in 1851 or over the century and a third it defended the trophy against all comers.

If the Eastern yachting establishment had ever wondered what it was like on the challengers' side of the Cup they got the chance after 1983, and the New York Yacht Club proved it could put on an equally impressive show from its new vantage point. The notion which has been suggested by some that the club had somehow grown weary of the tremendous and ever increasing responsibility of hosting the America's Cup lacks credibility given its aggressiveness to recover the Cup.

Having proven itself for so long, the New York Yacht Club's America II campaign had little difficulty in the high-priced sponsorship war among the six U.S. syndicates garnering the likes of Cadillac, Newsweek and Amway Corp., among others. The America II Challenge is organized and financed through the United States Merchant Marine Academy Foundation.

America II exhibited instant technique in the boasting game as well. Like other syndicates, especially sail America, America II made a great deal out of anything positive anyone had to say about its chances, especially if it came from an opposing syndicate. So while John Bertrand and other Australians were citing Conner as the man to beat, America II was making it well known that Bond's America's Cup Defence and the America's Cup Challengers Report had selected it to be the most likely group to defeat the Australian defender.

That's the way it was with several of the syndicates. Surveys, oddsmakers, stories and key syndicate officials were cited. Also, whenever a syndicate was the clear victor in any of the many trial races run before the eliminations, considerble public emphasis was placed on it. It was often quite difficult to determine which syndicates truly had the inside track for the Cup.

When Alan Bond, in his newsletter gave America II 3-1 odds to face the Australians, the syndicate was beside itself.

"Being recognized as the top competition by your opponent

is a phenomenal tribute. America II's *US-46* heightens our enthusiasm," said syndicate chairman chairman Richard DeVos. "It is the culmination of three years work by the best sailing and scientific minds in the United States. Its design evolved through extensive competitive testing of *US-42* and *US-44*, as well as from computer generated data and crew input."

For its part, America II never blushed at the praise. DeVos, agreed with all of it and added that America II would go on to defeat the Australian defender.

"Because we were the first U.S. challenger to train in Australia for the 1987 America's Cup we've gone to extraordinary lengths to gain an early and decisive edge in technology and experience," DeVos said.

The Data General Race Predictions Committee in Australia repeatedly ranked America II as one of the major threats to the Australians. The committee comprised mostly Aussies and therefore was arguably biased toward the Australians. Nevertheless several categories in its ratings chart reflected what the general concensus of sailors and oddsmakers were saying. Perhaps the real reason America II continued to give the Aussies goose bumps is that old traditions die hard, a justifiable attitude considering the New York Yacht Club's amazing 132-year winning streak.

New York Yacht Club Commodore Emil "Bus" Mosbacher Jr., who defended the Cup in 1962 and 1967, was equally direct.

"The club has been (was) home to the America's Cup for 132 consecutive years. We fully intend to return it to its righful home in the United States," Mosbacher said. (What about the British who struck the Cup and first offered it?)

The club was somewhat encouraged in February about its

prospects for the America's Cup when it took third place in the World 12-Meter Fleet Racing Championships. That's because *US-42* was only a trial boat and the syndicate knew that two new boats, *US-44* and *US-46*, were on the way. Additionally, numerous equipment problems were experienced during the racing and America II's final placing could have been higher if they hadn't occurred.

Bill Langan, head of America II's design team explained the thinking that went into *US-42*.

"At the start of the America II campaign, we knew we needed a trial horse to compare new designs against. We also knew that an existing hull would require changes to the structure, cockpit and rig for the heavy air conditions in Australia. Adding up the cost of buying an existing boat and making the necessary modifications, it didn't make sense to purchase a Newport-style 12-meter. Sure, we could have gone out sailing to see what the conditions were like. Instead, we decided to build our own trial horse and learn something extra. *US-42*, better known as Lego, earned her nickname because of her designed-in ability to change configurations. With Lego we were able to make gross changes to the boat, ranging from conventional to radical. We could see what we liked and didn't like in a very short period, trying out different keels, rudders, rig positions, displacements and rating configurations."

The heavier winds of Western Australia had been a key concern of designers as they poured over thousands of 12-meter drawings from 1983-86.

Yes, the Fremantle Doctor is to be taken seriously, Langan said, but he noted, "We're always treading a fine line between light enough and strong enough. Three of the America's Cup races in 1983 off Newport were decided by rigging failures:

Australia II's steering gear in the first race; *Australia II's* headboard carriage in the second race; and *Liberty's* jumper strut in race five."

After months of observation and arduous testing, the America II people had learned a great deal about what to expect at Fremantle.

"The rigs in Perth will be subjected to substantially higher loadings than they were in Newport, so we can probably expect each challenger to blow a rig at least once. The mast and all the fittings on the mast are being redesigned and re-engineered in order to give them sufficient strength, yet make them light enough to give the stability we need," he said.

Langan emphasized that *US-42* was strictly a trial horse. "She was never designed specifically to win the America's Cup. Most of the things we tried worked, and on any given day, we could win a race from the Australians. In *US-44* we have the boat necessary to beat them for the Cup."

In that case, the New York Yacht Club has two very capable boats because similar praise was heaped upon *US-46* when she was christened.

America II skipper John Kolius, 34, said after the christening that he believed *US-46*, not *44* would be the club's eventual entry and that was OK by him.

"*US-46* is the result of stringent research, daily testing and, in general, nitpicking by me and the crew. We are extremely pleased with the results . . . It's the culmination of more than two years of hard work, design and dedication and I believe this is the boat," Kolius said.

DeVos, always prepared to talk up the syndicate's chances, noted, "We have three of the fastest 12-meter yachts in the world, perhaps the finest crew ever assembled for international competition and more than 5,500 individual contributors working toward a single goal: to bring back the Cup."

At the top of the $15 million America II Challenge was 32-year Thomas F. Ehman Jr., the executive director He has raced competively since his boyhood, which had spent sailing on a small lake in Michigan. In 1986 he was the the current Narragansett Bay J-24 champion. He had won four North American championships, the U.S. Yacht Racing Union's Champion of Champions, was a former member of the national championship sailing team at the University of Michigan, past commodore of the Huron-Portage Yacht Club and the youngest international yacht racing judge in the world.

BNZ America's Cup Challenge

Challenge issued by: Royal New Zealand Yacht Squadron
Yachts: *KZ7*, *KZ5*, *KZ3*

Equipped with tons of fiberglass, the Kiwi contingent was hoping to sneak into Fremantle in October and quietly win the Louis Vuitton Cup, awarded to the eventual America's Cup challenger.

Unfortunately, they had already let the bird out of the cage eight months before at the Worlds where *KZ5* took second and was a model of consistency. New Zealand's finishes were first, third, fifth, third, third, seventh and third. The placings of the winning yacht, *Australia III*, were fourth, second, first, sixth, first, first, and she didn't compete in the seventh heat.

The New Zealanders were elated after their first time out.

"We were the new boys on the block when we arrived in

Perth. But look at the results: Our designers and sailors have certainly produced the goods," said Michael Fay, executive chairman for the BNZ America's Cup Challenge.

While the American groups and others were spending so much time on what they had to do to beat each other, the New Zealand threat was being overlooked. Had Australia not made it to the Worlds, the Royal New Zealand Yacht Squadron's bid would have seemed a lot more impressive and threatening to all of the challengers.

Not that the anyone was disregarding the "plastic fantastics" in Cup competition. There wasn't a rush after the Worlds to build fiberglass boats, but if New Zealand's latest twelve, *KZ7*, were to go on to win the America's Cup, the other syndicates, which concentrated so intently on winged keels for three years were perched to immerse themselves in what could become the latest revolution: building fiberglass twelves with winged keels.

The key premise behind the fiberglass boats is that they are stiffer longitudinally and therefore better able to withstand the rigors of the Fremantle chop, according to their designers Laurie Davidson, Bruce Farr, Russell Bowler and Ron Holland. Aluminum hulls flex considerably in the water, especially in a hefty chop, so the boat doesn't knife through the water as smoothly and evenly as a more rigid material.

Fiberglass hulls weren't the only innovations the Kiwis considered. New winged keel configurations were tested, the sail program was computerized, new types of rudders were tested and some say Holland may have come up with a breakthrough 12-meter mast, developed after 2,000 hours of design and testing.

The only challenges the Race Predictions Committee rated higher than New Zealand in June were Sail America and America

II.

If New Zealand's success in the Worlds wasn't enough to intimidate the others, the knowledge that the Kiwi crew was rated by the Predications Committee to be the best among the challengers and equal to Australia's best, the crew of *Australia III*, should have been sufficient to earn them new respect. Not everyone gave the crew such high marks but few disputed that the New Zealanders' motivation was at a high going into the eliminations.

BNZ Challenge made much of the fact that Dennis Conner had remarked in a visit to Auckland for *KZ7's* launching that he believed the final four challengers probably would include the New Zealanders as well as the others previously mentioned.

At 24, BNZ skipper Chris Dickson was probably the best skipper in the world in his age group, and could be the one additional plus New Zealand would need in its quest to snatch up the Cup on its first try. In addition to helming *KZ5* to a second in the Worlds, Dickson had a string of wins and high finishes in a diverse seven-year sailing career that had seen him sail in a wide range of classes and helm a variety of boats, including one-tons, ultra-lights, twelves and many others.

The BNZ Challenge, which cost an estimated $16 million, was spearheaded in 1984 by the Auckland banking firm of Fay, Richwhite. Soon after a group of New Zealanders decided to make a bid for the Cup, the company, which has offices in Sydney and London, became a prime mover in the campaign.

The principal sponsor in the Cup bid was the Bank of New Zealand, hence the name BNZ Challenge.

Challenge KIS France

Challenge issued by: Yacht Club de Sete
Yachts: *French Kiss, Freedom, Enterprise*

The *Kiss* was still a *Kiss* when the racing began at the Worlds, despite the protestations of the Royal Perth Yacht Club before the first heat.

The Royal Perth contended the *French Kiss* violated the International Yacht Racing Union's rule 26, which prohibits the use of commericial names on yachts in some classes, in this case the America's Cup.

The yacht belongs to the KIS syndicate. KIS is an acronym for Key Instant Service. The company dates back to July 1963 when its founder, entrepreneur Serge Crasnianski just happened to lose his keys. He was unhappy to learn it would take several days to have new ones made. The following month he began his first instant key services company. Crasnianski did a little branching out and today he maintains that "KIS is number one worldwide in the field of photo minilabs, holding 60 percent of the American market share and 50 percent in Japan." Add to that instant engraving, hot-foil printing, instant shoe repair, color photo copiers, and medical equipment like the KIS portable blood laboratory. At last count KIS was in more than 50 foreign countries, and had subsidiaries in 28 states of the United States.

Crasnianski didn't arrive where he is today by passing up promising opportunities but it remains uncertain how much of an advertising scheme he had in mind when *French Kiss* was named. The uproar initiated by the Royal Perth, however, ensured Crasnianski and KIS an advertising campaign that would have cost millions.

Magic and Eagle   Courtesy of Eagle Challenge

On Feb. 6, an international rules jury, which had convened for the Worlds ruled the name didn't infringe on rule 26. There was a great outcry over the ruling and many predicted the logos of sponsors would sail the seas on the burgees and sails of racing yachts. While there are some classes of yachting where advertising on sails is commonplace the practice hasn't become widespread since the KIS ruling. None of the dozen or so America's Cup twelves constructed after the Worlds had followed suit by late 1986.

Mostly smiles greet *French Kiss'* tender, the boat which escorts her in and out each day. *Kiss Me Tender*, however, grabbed a few headlines herself.

French Kiss probably wouldn't have captured quite so many headlines had she been a mediocre or incompetent performer, but she was neither.

Under the guidance of one of France's highest paid athletes, helmsman Marc Pajot, a world-class sailor and Olympic medalist, she came in fifth place at the Worlds, but more importantly she won two of the seven heats and took second in another.

Shortly after that regatta, in trials against America II, *French Kiss* held her own. In five match races at Fremantle against New Zealand, she won four, leaving the KIS clan with smiles on their faces. Their boat had proved itself against some of the best 12-meters. In one of *French Kiss'* wins at the Worlds, *Australia III* didn't race, but in the other win it wasn't that Bond's boat had a poor race — it came in second. Riding high, *French Kiss* went home to undergo a few changes to make her even better.

Prior to the Cup series, *French Kiss* generally performed pretty much as her designer Philippe Briande had intended, as a heavy-weather yacht. He gave her a lot of volume up front and in her aft, but that forced her to go with a smaller sail area in order to comply with the 12-meter rule.

French Kiss has been characterized as being "schizophrenic." That might appear to be true if her placings in the Worlds are considered, but the wind variable also must be taken into account.

She finished ninth in the first race but light-to-medium winds that freshened during the race fell off in the latter stages.

In race two, she went out in front in a 20-knot wind and stayed in front as the breeze built until an equipment problem slowed her down. Nevertheless, the strong wind held and she beat *Australia III* by 52 seconds.

After her victory in the previous race, *French Kiss* finished an unlikely sixth in medium to heavy weather, but she had equipment problems early and they hampered her performance much of the way.

The rest of the regatta reads much the same way on the *French Kiss* scorecard. There were times when she seemed to fly past the other twelves, leaving opposing crew members astonished.

Before the Worlds, Crasnianski had seriously considered building a second boat but discarded the notion after he saw *French Kiss* perform, opting instead to optimize her existing features and try to improve her light-air capability.

If heavy weather were to prevail in Fremantle — and that is normal for the latter and earlier parts of the year — there was a good possibility *French Kiss* would be the challenger facing the Australian defender.

Golden Gate Challenge

Challenge issued by: St. Francis Yacht Club
Yacht: *USA*

Any discussion of Golden Gate Challenge's 1987 Cup bid would not be properly presented unless it included *USA* skipper Tom Blackaller's famous declaration of his camp's two major goals while in the land Down Under.

"We don't just want the Cup, we want the whole damned island." Blackaller stated.

Knowing Blackaller's rather candid, colorful and charismatic ways, the Australians took these bold remarks with a sporting sense of humor. Just the same, the Aussies were on the lookout for him to make certain he left their island continent empty-handed on both counts.

Although there were numerous assertions of innovation and radicalness as new twelves were turned out at a furious pace in 1986, the Golden Gate Challenge was only one of two syndicates — the other was the British America's Cup Challenge — to proclaim they had constructed "revolutionary" boats, and the term isn't used lightly these days, not since the wings of *Australia II*. In the world of twelves the term has only been applied to her winged keel and the rudder-keel configuration of *Intrepid* in 1967.

Restating something else Blackaller said earlier, since his words were liable to reverberate loudly in the ears of the other contenders, "What we're doing is creating the fastest America's Cup racer in sailing history . . . from concept through construction . . . and frankly we're going to blow everyone out of the water."

Blackaller proved during the six months prior to the trials

that he was as adept at stirring up curiousity as he was at steering a twelve. There was considerable speculation over what it was the syndicate had come up with, most people assuming it was on the order of a new keel configuration. A month before the first round-robin series the rumor, though it had not been confirmed, was that Golden Gate designers had devised a keel with two underwater spars joined by a torpedo-shaped lead bulb. Whether such a configuration actually represented a revolution depended entirely on *USA's* performance, if indeed that is what the design team had developed. As for revealing the keel, Golden Gate seemed perfectly content for as long as it could get away with it to avoid revealing or even discussing the "revolution" in any meaningful detail.

The Golden Gate Challenge put together one of the most technologically oriented design teams in its quest for the Cup, from its computer wizard, physicist Heiner Meldner, who took leave from his work on Star Wars, to naval architect-designer Gary Mull and Alberto Calderon, an aerodynamicist and hydrodynamicist.

On somewhat of a prophetic note, Golden Gate pointed out that *Australia II* skipper and sailmaker John Bertrand and sailmaker Tom Schnachenberg, were employees of the first sailmaker to use computer-designed sails by Meldner.

With respect to the sails, hull mast and everything else on a 12-meter boat, Meldner said, "We want to jump years ahead and come up with a computer simulation that will advance the current state-of-the-art of yacht design by many years. We want to win. We have technological advantages over the other challengers, like supercomputers, the computer programs that go with them, and the people who know how to use this combination successfully."

Mull brought to the team design expertise which included work on the 12-meter *Constellation*, a slew of winning 6-meter yachts, the *Ranger 37*, *Improbable* and a new class of vessel for the Navy.

Calderon, an internationally known consultant in aerospace research added wing and vehicle design experience to the team. His assignment was to reduce as much as possible hydrodynamic resistance, or drag, on the boat.

The Race Predictions Committee in April had *USA* rated sixth best among all contenders. Since the defense ratings wouldn't matter until and if *USA* reached the finals, the rating among challengers was more important. Golden Gate came in fourth among challengers, behind Sail America, America II and New Zealand.

Two months later the Predictions Committee dropped Golden Gate's rating points and that bumped the syndicate down to fifth among challengers with Newport Beach's Eagle Challenge taking over the fourth spot.

How much do such ratings mean at race time? Over a long period, perhaps the numbers might be borne out. If, however, a boat should lose its bowman in a short series of races, its rigging fails, or any one of several dozen other things goes wrong, the ratings can be thrown out for that particular boat. It's liable to go out in the next race and out-sail all of the others.

Until a boat is seen under race conditions, its ability "to blow everyone out of the water" remains questionable and the same can be said for skippers.

Unquestionably, Blackaller can tack with the very best. He has been tested and proved himself to be in strong contention as one of the world's top sailors. He's been racing competitively

USA

since 1951 and holds a number of records. His post has mostly been at the helm in contests such as the Bermuda Race, the Transpac, SORC and Fasnet races. In 1983 he skippered *Defender* in the Cup trials but lost out to Conner and *Liberty*. He is a two-time World Star Class Champion, 6-meter world champion and winner of the Clipper Cup and Sardinia Cup. A month before the Worlds he took first place in the American-Australian Challenge Cup 6-meter race in Sydney. He is also a successful race-car driver, once finishing fourth in the 12-hour Sebring and fifth in the 24-hour Daytona.

Eagle Challenge

Challenge issued by: Newport Harbor Yacht Club
Yachts: *Eagle, Magic*

The *Eagle* will fly, or at least sail at a pretty good clip, its well-known chief designer, Johan Valentijn, believed after the boat was constructed.

Eagle president Gary Thomson said the boat's keel is "a breakthrough, radical design that is visible to the eye." (Note the term, revolutionary, was not used.)

Valentijn didn't make any bold claims about how the boat would sail the keels off of all the rest, but he was pleased with *Eagle*, the flagship of the Newport Harbor Yacht Club's Eagle Challenge, which hails from Newport Beach, Calif.

"I'm quite confident in the new boat, and I'm quite confident in our skipper, Rod Davis. Some people might describe what we've done with our keel as rather risky. I don't feel that way. Rather than call the keel a breakthrough now, I'd just as soon

wait and let *Eagle's* performance on the water do the talking,"
Valentijn said.

Davis, 30, of Coronado, Calif., has the credentials for taking
the wheel of any sailing ship but chose the *Eagle*, which weighs
23 tons, is 65 feet long and cost more than $1 million to design
and build.

Davis is a four-time world champion, Olympic gold medalist
in sailing, two-time Congressional Cup winner, and a superior
match racer.

Winged keels, breakthroughs, revolutionary concepts, are
well and good, but, said Davis, "Just give me and the crew a
quality boat — it doesn't have to be the fastest — and I think
we can win it all."

Thomson likes that kind of talk, especially in light of of a
study by Chapman College in Orange, Calif., which concluded
that 4,300 jobs could be created in Southern California if the
Cup were there, and 1.6 million additional tourists would be
attracted to the area.

Davis is an optimist and has the talent — if he has the
boat — to win the Cup, but he was more reserved than some
in his predictions for the final outcome.

"I have no doubt the United States will win back the Cup
in '87. Whether it's Dennis Conner, or John Kolius or us, I can't
say 100 percent for sure. But the *Eagle* has all the right players.
The Australians won't know what hit them. It will be like
waking the sleeping giant. The *Eagle* has the opportunity and
it's the thrill of a lifetime," Davis said.

If Valentijn's breakthrough keel and Davis' capability weren't
quite enough to get the job done, the Southern California group
hoped the impressive depiction of a fierce-looking eagle in flight
on the side of the boat would provide some additional wing

power. Unlike some of the other syndicates, which tried two or more boats out before making a final decision on which to run, the Newport Beach group decided early on that the *Eagle* and nothing but the *Eagle* is what this challenge would go with. To ensure Davis and his crew some match-racing practice in their new boat, the syndicate purchased Magic. Because of its similarities to *Australia II*, Magic also proved to be a valuable aid to Valentijn in his design of the new hull. Valentijn's interest and dabbling with winged keels goes as far back as most who have experimented with them, and he spent considerable time with the Newport Beach group searching for the perfect one to fit on *Eagle's* underside.

While the Eagle Challenge, one of the late arrivals to 1987 Cup competition, couldn't boast quite the extravagant technological input into its boat that rival syndicates to the north and south could, some assistance was lent by McDonnell Douglas and its Unigraphics II computer. Boeing experts were also in on the project and aided Valentijn in producing the new 12-meter yacht.

Heart of America Challenge

Challenge issued by: Chicago Yacht Club
Yachts: *Heart of America, Defender, Clipper*

It wasn't exactly at the eleventh hour, but waiting until May 1986 to get its first twelve and a crew out on the water was pushing it considering the two or three-boat headstart other syndicates had on the Chicago Yacht Club's Heart of America Challenge.

What's that? Did he say Chicago? Well sink me. Isn't that in the Midwest or someplace?

Indeed it is, but Chicago attorney Jordan H. Peters was so persuasive in his pitch to the New York State Supreme Court he all but had the Windy City on the Atlantic Coast.

The first order of Heart-of-America business was to make sure Chicago qualified to be a host city under the Cup's Deed of Gift. The deed specifies that challengers must "hold their regattas on the sea or an arm of the sea."

The court agreed with Peters' argument that Chicago qualified to be a host city because it is a port of Lake Michigan.

So?

Well, argued Peters, "There is international navigation of the Great Lakes, Chicago is an international port, and marine life comes into the Great Lakes from the ocean." — ergo.

Heart of America attorneys also noted that the Marine Act of 1970 established the Great Lakes as the fourth seacoast of the United States.

The Supreme Court went for it. There could be America's Cup racing in Chicago.

Huh?

It's only right and proper that it should be there, explains *Heart of America* skipper Buddy Melges, the man people remind you about if you dare to suggest someone else is the best skipper in the world.

"For kangaroos, koalas and waltzing Matilda, Australia is fine, but I think any cup called America belongs not only in America, but in the Heart of America," said Melges. (What about England?)

Sailors in the Midwest? Huh?

That's right, said Melges, "Sailors in the Midwest are as

good as any, and a lot more people are going to know it by the time 1987 is over."

Heart of America, or *US 51*, has the following specifications: white aluminum hull with an outline of the Great Lakes; 65 feet long, 45 feet at the waterline; overall weight, 65,000 pounds, including her 40,000-pound ballast and her 15,000-pound keel; 90-foot mast; cost, including sail rig, almost $1.7 million; and an inventory of 190 sails.

James Gretzky, project coordinator for the Heart of America design team, said the syndicate had an edge over the rest of the state-side contenders in one respect. "The Naval Ship Research and Development Center in Maryland (where the boat's tank's tests were conducted) is technologically superior to the tank-testing facilities being used by other U.S. syndicates, which gives Heart of America a tremendous competitive advantage. There is more precision, accuracy and reproducibility with a larger facility, so we should be able to avoid some of the problems with small scale models," Gretzky explained.

Melges and the Heart of America team, which spent more than $7 million on the campaign — modest compared to most of the others — prided themselves on their openness in challenge matters, including *US 51*, which proudly displayed her keel at a showing in Newport. Several of the syndicates have been using guard dogs and security officers. One reportedly had a former FBI agent and a former CIA agent to handle security matters. Usually, it's not the bow or backsides they're looking out for, but their undersides, such is the interest and paranoia these days over winged keels.

Not so with *Heart of America*. There she was, her winged keel on display for all to see. "If they copy our keel, Melges said, "they can only get as good a boat as ours, and we should

160

be able to beat them with our intelligence of the rig that comes with the boat."

All that about sailing on Lake Michigan and the goodness of Heart of America's heart is fine, but what about the boat, the crew? Could they win?

Melges, who at 56 is the senior America's Cup skipper among those who are still pursuing it, seemed to think so.

After sailing his new boat around Narragansett Bay off Rhode Island, Melges had this to say: "It's amazing. I've heard stories of winged keels making boats gyrate all over the sea, but this one is tracking as nicely as Clipper (the well-known Chicago twelve that was used to train the crew) with her set trim-tab. She sails for half a mile without me touching the wheel. She sails free at her own pace and just walks into the wind."

He also liked his crew's chances and said sailors, not boats, would make the difference. "Apart from the development in sails and rig, it's going to come down to the men and the boys with their toys."

Perhaps. If it is the sailor who will make the difference, many will lay odds Melges is the one to do it.

A sailmaker and boatbuilder from Zenda, Wis., Melges is another world-class champion sailor. Over the past 25 years he has won: a gold medal in the Soling class at the 1972 Olympics; a bronze in the flying Dutchman class in the 1964 games; the Star World Championships in 1978 and 1979; as well as many other U.S. and North American contests in scows, Solings and other one-design boats in 25 years of competition. Additionally, Melges has been named Yachtsman of the year three times, and is the only skipper ever to win the U.S. Sailing Championship's Mallory Cup three times in a row.

1986–1987 America's Cup Program

LOUIS VUITTON CUP	DEFENDERS CUP

ROUND ROBINS

Round Robin 1	October 5 - 20
Round Robin 2	November 2 - 19
Round Robin 3	December 2 - 19

Each yacht meets the others once in each Round Robin

SEMI-FINALS

December 28 - January 7

The four top-scoring yachts enter the semi-finals.

First yacht vs fourth

Second yacht vs third

The first yacht of each pair to win four races advances to the final

LOUIS VUITTON CUP FINALS

January 13–23

The winner of the Louis Vuitton Cup is the one to first win four races. This cup winner than meets the best defender in the America's Cup Challenge itself

SERIES

Series A	October 18 - 30
Series B	November 10 - 23
Series C	December 4 - 19
Series D	December 29 - January 10

Each yacht meets the others twice in each Series

The two top-scoring yachts enter the final

DEFENDERS CUP FINALS

January 16–25

The winner defends the America's Cup against the Louis Vuitton Cup winner

1987 AMERICA'S CUP FINALS

Challengers versus Defender

January 31 – February 12

162

Courageous Challenge

Challenge issued by: Yale Corinthian Yacht Club
Yachts: *Courageous IV*, *Defender*

For much of 1986 it didn't appear *Courageous* would return to the America's Cup or that the yacht would have a syndicate strong enough to withstand the financial and organizational problems forever threatening to destroy Cup campaigns.

Winner of the Cup in 1974 and 1977, Courageous' retirement from Cup racing seemed inevitable when the old campaigner sailed to a disappointing 12th in a field of 14 at the Worlds in February, never doing better than eighth in the seven heats.

At the helm of *Courageous* during the Worlds was Peter Isler, who quit the syndicate four months later primarily because it was decided not to build a new boat. Isler said he thought he had the crew to wage a good challenge, and he only needed a competitive boat to have a chance. He had only been with the syndicate since late 1985. The helm was vacant for about a year before Isler was named.

The syndicate named its vice president, sailmaker Dave Vietor, to replace Isler at the helm.

Said Norman Rosenblum, the syndicate's administrative coordinator, Vietor "has been a skipper, navigator and coordinator of several campaigns. David has the knack for pushing a group in the right direction. He also has the ability to pull the varied personalities involved in this challenge together and get the most out of the sailors as well as the boat."

Meanwhile, adjustments to the keel and rigging apparently corrected a balance problem, which may have accounted for Courageous' dismal effort in the Worlds.

Courageous is a boat of the middle 1970s, born at a time when 12-meter yachts were created on paper, not computer monitors.

With new vortex wings at least giving *Courageous* the semblance of a boat of the 1980s and the rah-rahs of her sponsor, the Yale Corinthian Yacht Club, to cheer her on, perhaps a two-time Cup winner can merge past and present for a final grand showing. The oddsmakers didn't see it that way at all and generally picked *Courageous* to finish near the back of the pack.

Canada's Challenge for the America's Cup

Challenge issued by: Royal Nova Scotia Yacht Squadron
Yachts: *Canada II*, *True North*

True North, the Royal Nova Scotia Yacht Squadron's entry in the Worlds, didn't fair too badly, coming in sixth out of the 14 vessels entered. Then the club got together with the Secret Cove Yacht Club and both discovered that united they were much stronger than apart and, better still, Secret Cove's twelve, *Canada I*, was faster than *True North*.

Less than three months after the Worlds, the two Canadian syndicates decided the Cup was more attainable together and they completed the merger. They joined forces, and Secret Cove's boat, which was renamed *Canada II* after refurbishment, proved to be the faster of the two after a long series of run-offs between them.

Guarding against a rift that might result from wounded pride, the two groups came up with the idea of sailing under the burgee of the club whose boat had been rejected, though *True North* also made the trip to serve as trial horse. The idea seemed to please most concerned, so the official challenger for the Canadians would be the Royal Nova Scotia Yacht Club, amd the syndicate name is, Canada's Challenge for the America's cup. Canadian citizens who were interested in the matter generally seemed to like the idea of the merger, the peaceful process that brought it about, and most of all that the country now had a viable and financially healthy challenge for the Cup.

Canada has had only three Cup experiences: The first two were the unmentionable bids in 1876 by the Countess of Dufferin and in 1881 by Atalanta; the third was of the more pleasant variety when *Canada I* surprised itself and everyone else by making it to the semi-finals of the historic 1983 challenger series.

Canada II made the long journey to Fremantle aboard the ocean liner, Nedlloyd Kembla, via Los Angeles where she was to pick up *Eagle* about in the third week of July stop also was planned in Hawaii where the Sail America armada was to be loaded. The twelves were scheduled to arrive in the third week of August, but didn't dock until early September. Soon afterward *Canada II* was due to spar against *Eagle* as the two syndicates had agreed to do in order to be primed for the October trials. While not all of the syndicates were so friendly toward one another, there were some like these two who it would be advantageous to race against some the Cup twelves.

After *Canada II's* arrival, her able helmsman, Terry Neilson, was ready to get out on the water and start the racing. "Right now we're as fit as any other crew. Our grinders are a match for anybody even at this stage," Neilson said. It was no wonder considering that the crew's daily fitness schedule includes 10 kilometers of roadwork, 90 minutes of weight training, 35 kilometers of cycling, and aerobics and other gymnasium work.

Before leaving home, syndicate officials estimated the Canadians would need about 36 wins, 32 in the trials and four in the finals, to take the America's Cup to Canada. Prior to the Canadian merger, the Data Race Predictions Committee had *True North* as the sixth best among the challenge hopefuls, but *Canada II* was ranked only 12th best. Nevertheless, Neilson and his crew, not quite as experienced as some of the others, expressed confidence, especially after the boat's excellent performance in June off Santa Cruz, Calif., against *True North* and *Heart of America*. Wind conditions there were fairly heavy and the Canadians were hoping they were representative of Fremantle's wind and sea conditions. If so they believed *Canada II* had a very good shot. It must also be remembered that *Canada II* is actually an updated *Canada I*, the boat that made it to the semifinals in the 1983 Cup challenges at Newport. Her modernization, one of the most extensive for any of the existing boats, included addition of a winged keel, a longer waterline, a new bow and stern and a new deck layout.

Despite not having every one of the stock components you might expect in a legitimate challenge, the Canadians, like the Kiwis, possessed that most unpredictable commodity, a high level of enthusiasm, particularly after the neat way the two syndicates had come together. The Canadians hoped to be the surprise for this match-up.

British America's Cup Challenge

Challenge issued by: Royal Thames Yacht Club
Yachts: *Crusader II (White Crusader), Crusader I*

Comes *Crusader II*, the "Hippo," and her declaration to the field as she pounds and pushes through the Fremantle chop: "Rule Britannia!" Such has been the dream of British sailors the past 136 years. Afterall, they made the blasted thing — the Cup by rights, was theirs. And didn't the silver trophy long for its home along the Thames.

As true and touching as all that may be, to make the dream come, Harold Cudmore, skipper, sailing manager and syndicate director has to get past some pretty stiff competition at the wheel of *Crusader II*, Britain's latest twelve.

With a calling card like Cudmore's, a hippo might be enough. Six times, he won the Royal Lymington Cup, Britain's match-racing championship, and he has won the Australia Cup, MAXI Yacht World Championship and dozens of other important races.

Cudmore believed when he received the new boat the that she was much more than a hippo of much more than a hippo and explained why while assessimg some basic pre-race tactics by comparing 1983 with 1987.

"Off Newport, R.I., in 1983, Alan Bond's *Australia II* won against the Americans because she was radically different (from) all the other yachts. This time, the Australians are concentrating on developing that winning concept. They seem to be leaving innovation to the challengers," Cudmore said.

"I believe *Crusader II* represents the technological breakthrough needed to bring the Cup home to Britain after an interval of 136 years. In *Crusader II* we have innovation. In Crusader (hippo's predecessor) we have the peak of conventional 12-meter design. Perhaps most important of all, we have the most experienced match-race crew in the world. Our chances have never looked better," he said.

From the royal tongue of Charles, the Prince of Wales, came the message: "The racing is clearly going to be as fiercely contested as ever, with a number of highly professional teams trying to wrest the Cup from its new home in Fremantle (actually, your Grace, the Cup is in Perth), but I am confident that our challenge has the organization, design skills and sailing ability to win. (And lest ye forget) if we do, the benefits will be substantial, not just in terms of national pride but in the business and jobs which would be generated by defending the America's Cup in this country." Prince Charles is commodore of the Royal Thames Yacht Club.

On the subject of secrecy, Cudmore explained that his people weren't as paranoid as some of the others, but he fudged a little by adding, "But *Crusader II* is something special. We can't afford to give away the secrets of her revolutionary design. This is particularly true because the Australians have just altered the rules in their own favor. We have to decide by October which boat will represent Britain, but the Australians can now leave a decision on the defending boat until December, after they have studied the (challenger) elimination races. We need to keep K-25's secrets up our sleeve for as long as possible."

Consorzio Azzurra Sfide Italiana America's Cup

Challenge issued by: Yacht Club Costa Smeralda
Yachts: — *Azzurra IV*, *Azzurra III*, *Azzurra II*, *Azzurra I*

The Azzurra challenge held the distinction of being the challenger of record for the 1987 America's Cup.

Shortly after the 1983 series, Yacht Club Costa Smeralda issued a challenge for a Cup race in 1987. It was the first club to issue a challenge and the distinction meant it to take on the enormous task of organizing and running the challenge races from Oct. 5 through Jan. 23.

The man who had to take on such a large responsibility is Com.te Gianfranco Alberini, commodore of the Yacht Club Costa Smeralda. Regarded as an excellent yachtsman himself, the rest of the America's Cup challenge slate anticipated he would organize a first-rate challenge program in Fremantle. The friendly Alberini represented the Italian navy internationally and won the Brest-Canary Island race of 1957.

The yacht club's role of host was the major distinction for the Sardinia contingent going into the challenge series, because its success on the water had been limited, since the 1983 Cup, especially in its disappointing 10th place finish in the Worlds. Azzurra did, however, do a lot of observing at the regatta and learned that a more innovative boat would be prerequisite to returning to Fremantle eight months later for the October challenge trials.

Unlike some of the others, the Azzurra campaign didn't suffer from a lack of funds — an estimated $25 million was spent. That's because large, wealthy corporate sponsors, like Fiat, have been there as well as the Aga Khan, to ensure the

Sardinia-based group's continuation.

When he's not busy as the spiritual leader of 12 million Shia Ismaili Moslems worldwide, the Aga Khan, head of the syndicate's presidential committee and one of the wealthiest individuals in the world, concerns himself with race horses, his luxurious European summer resort in Sardinia and extensive business interests. The syndicate is commited to steadily improving its capabilities until 1991, the year helmsman Mauro Pelashier predicted the Azzurra syndicate will win the America's Cup. Costa Smeralda set out in 1981 on a 10-year program designed to result in a Mediterranean-based America's Cup meet. Pelashier made his declaration six months before the Worlds, an experience which sobered the aspirations of some with the syndicate.

While Azzurra was performing in a lackluster style, the syndicate was greatly impressed at the Worlds with the boats of the New Zealand contingent, which Bond characterized as the true winners of the regatta. Later in 1986 the Italian group set about with plans to build a fiberglass boat of its own but time grew short and it was decided the fourth Azzurra would be of aluminum.

Cino Ricci, the skipper of Azzurra at the 1983 America's Cup when the group made such an impressive showing for its first time out, had to give up his position to Lorenzo Bortolotti, who resigned from the other Italian syndicate because he wasn't given enough decision-making authority. Ricci became the group's general consultant and then later was put in charge of the feasibility study for the third boat. Pelaschier was assigned to continue as Azzurra helmsman, which in this case meant he would steer the boat — what the syndicate calls a skipper is actually someone who calls the shots along the lines of a tactician.

It was questionable whether the Azzurra bid could possibly enjoy the kind of success it did in 1983, both because the competition — crews and boats — just may be the best ever assembled for an America's Cup, and because the syndicate waited so long to turn out *Azzurra IV*, perhaps not allowing sufficient time for testing, fine tuning and crew training aboard an unfamiliar boat. The new boat was so tardy plans were made to have it flown by jumbo jet to Fremantle.

Corsorzio Italia

Challenge issued by: Yacht Club Italio
Yachts: *Italia II, Italia, Victory'83*

Consorzio Italia was still riding high in February 1986 at Fremantle as its boat, *Italia*, prepared to race in the World 12-Meter Fleet Racing Championships.

That's because the syndicate was the reigning Worlds champ, having sailed *Victory'83* to a first-place finish in the previous contest, which was run in June 1984 at Porto Cervo in Sardinia. The regatta featured the likes of Conner, Kolius, Davis, Pajot and Blackaller — an excellent preview of the 1987 America's Cup. In the finals it was an all-Italian performance, *Victory'83* versus *Azzurra*. The contest went down to the final race but it ended with the former Britisher, *Victory'83*, coming in on top. The Italians, so new to the heavyweight matchups in the world of twelves, were making believers out of the rest of the field.

Then, like its countrymen from Sardinia, the Genoa-based

Consorzio *Italia* faltered. The 1986 Worlds had severly dampened the Gucci-clad gang, which finished in a less-than-mediocre ninth place.

In the fray, Flavio Scala and his crew learned that Fremantle can be cruel even if you are nicely dressed. In race five, the water was exceptionally choppy as winds ranged from 18-25 knots. Bowman Lorenzo Mazza had been gathering in a headsail on the fourth leg when he was dumped over the side. He was fished out by a safety boat. Since the crew didn't recover its man unassisted, the boat wasn't allowed to finish the race and the *Italia* was assessed a costly 21 points, effectively ruining its chances for a reasonable finish in the regatta. In the seventh race Mazza got a second dose of Fremantle saltwater and teammate Stefano Maida followed him into the drink. It was a rough Worlds for the syndicate. The reaction of syndicate officials was to return to the drawing board. The result was *Italia* II.

The construction was completed in June, but *Italia II* had a disastrous beginning and members of Yacht Club Italiano nearly had heart attacks when they learned that soon after her christening *Italia II* was forced 6 meters underwater when a heavy crane collapsed while lowering her in the harbor at La Spezia southeast of Genoa. The boat was pumped out and taken to an Adriatic Coast shipyard to recover from the near disaster and to be made ready for the trials in Fremantle. More than a month was lost, and like her countrymen with the Azzurra campaign the Corsorzio Italia crew lost precious training time because of the mishap.

It remained uncertain for much of 1986 just who would steer *Italia II* in Fremantle. The very capable Scala had expressed some discontent with Doctor Fremantle, as some of the Italians term it. While it appeared that Scala was desirous of being a sparring partner he remained the official choice through much of 1986 while the syndicate considered others as potential skippers, including Roberto Chieffi, who helmed *Victory'83* in the 1986 Worlds. Shortly before the challenger trials, however, A. Migliaccio was listed as Consorzio Italia's lead skipper.

The disarray in too many categories at the eleventh hour may have destined the Consorzio Italia for further disappointment before 1986 was out. Still, having tasted big-league 12-meter success at the 1984 Worlds, and apparently not being faced with much of a financial limitation, it appeared the syndicate would be a Cup participant for many series to come.

Challenge France

Challenge issued by: Societe Nautique de Marseilles
Yachts: *Challenge France, Challenge 12, France 3*

Challenge France made an heroic effort to stay afloat throughout much of 1986 and in the end succeeded in keeping its bid for the America's Cup alive, but not until after it had filed for bankruptcy.

The Marseilles syndicate all but withdrew from the Worlds in February because of financial difficulties which plagued it the syndicate and precluded even the basic costs for keeping a twelve in the water and a crew in training.

It appeared in June the Cup bid had gone under for the third time when the syndicate filed for bankruptcy protection. A major problem, one that syndicates in other nations have had, was that Challenge France was competing for the same sponsors as rival Challenge KIS and the latter was winning.

Challenge France skipper Yves Pajot, whose brother Marc Pajot helms for the more southerly based KIS campaign, remained optimistic during the first half of the year and confident that if the campaign were rejuvenated he and his crew could get in shape in time for the October trials.

Money was so tight, the training program for Challenge France was halted at the beginning of 1986 and the campaign floundered about until June and bankruptcy. The syndicate had been written off by practically everyone, including officials in Fremantle who didn't expect the group to make an appearance.

Then a benefactor surfaced in the form of Grundig, the German electronics manufacturer. Other groups with a few francs pitched in enough of them to get the campaign and a new twelve designed by Daniel Andrieu back in the water in time for the October trials. The boat was launched in July and shipped to Fremantle in August.

Whether Yves Pajot, who believed technology would be the key to victory in Australia, and his crew would be sharp enough to sail with the best in the world remained a legitimate concern right up to the trials.

The syndicate did try to catch up a little by employing some of France's heavyweights in design technology when the new boat was undertaken, including the French space agency. Pajot may at least have come up with a competitive boat to work with. Also, having purchased Challenge 12, designed by none other than Ben Lexcen, the syndicate had a fairly sophisticated plan from which it could begin work on the new twelve.

Challenge France knew going in it would be a long shot for 1987 and may have viewed the whole affair as more of an attempt to gain the experience and exposure needed to mount a serious challenge a few years down the road.

Fremantle and Newport Course Comparison

The instructions to designers and builders of 12-meter yachts for the 1987 America's Cup: Build boats that can take a little roughing-up in the heavy weather and seas off the coast of Western Australia.

It was a response to the widespread uncertainty over what to expect out of something the locals in Fremantle and Perth affectionately and reverently referred to as the "Fremantle Doctor." The name refers to the strong southwesterlies that blow in the afternoons from approximately December to March.

The uncertainty stemmed from the uncharacteristic weather at the Worlds February 1986. The regatta was supposed to be a preview of the 1987 America's Cup because most of the syndicates and yachts entered would be common to both contests, and they would be racing over the same general course area at approximately the same time of year. The only problem was that instead of experiencing the normal blow of the place, what they got was an imposter; the Doctor did kick up now and then but it turned out to be a record-breaking February for passivity. There were times when some of the heavier yachts appeared frozen on the sea.

After the Worlds there were some rather important questions on the minds of those who had participated and those who had observed from afar: Now what kind of boat do we build? Would the Doctor return for the elimination races and the finals of the America's Cup? What's it really like when the Doctor is in?

Better not take any risks, the syndicates decided, so they compromised by building yachts they hoped would sail effectively in light or heavy weather — if they succeeded it would be somewhat of a 12-meter design milestone. The compromise meant the possibility of having to do a number of things, including adding length for stability, including more freeboard space between the water and deck, more durable equipment on board and designing hulls that could sit a little higher on the water. The longer hulls, more freeboard and other changes would necessitate adjustments elsewhere on the boat in order to comply with the 12-meter formula; effectively that meant reduction in sail area. It all resulted in some significant changes in the appearance as well as the performance of 12-meter yachts compared to what they looked like and how they performed at Newport in 1983.

In Newport, sailors had to contend with large sea swells most of the time, and huge swells in a strong wind. Sailing amid these swells was far less taxing on the boats and the crew than sailing in the harsher conditions at Fremantle.

In Fremantle, there is not so much a swell action as there is a chop. Off the coast, almost due east about 13 miles, is Rottnest Island and some coral outcroppings just south of there. This island land mass acts as a wind and sea buffer because the course is on a straight line with the island and the major winds of the area, a southwesterlies. The various influences of these southwesterlies, plus winds from other directions and the bodies of land, including the Australian continent to the east, serve to create frequent short, choppy waves on the course.

The boats therefore sail in a constant up-and-down motion

and this causes considerable strain on the sails and rigging, but especially on the sailors as demonstrated in the Worlds when several bowmen were swept overboard. What was particularly scary to some who participated in the regatta was the thought that normal conditions were considerably harsher; that could mean frequent, possibly consistent southwesterly wind speeds of 25-30 knots, which would be stronger than any conditions ever recorded for an America's Cup series.

In one of the 1962 races at Newport, the yacht, *Weatherly*, faced *Gretel* in north and west winds that ranged from 22 to 28 miles per hour, or 19.1-24.3 knots. That, however, was for a single race. The America's Cup had always been sailed in far milder conditions than those predicted for Fremantle.

Challengers and defenders were relieved in mid-1986 when the Fremantle Port Authority, Royal Perth Yacht Club and Costa Smeralda Yacht Club — the challenger of record — all agreed to the use of alternative race courses during the elimination series in the event there should be strong southwesterlies on a given day. Spectators were all for the plan since use of the alternate courses would bring the yachts much closer to the shore, and in the case of one, to within about 750 meters, a spectator's dream.

The same parties that agreed to the alternate courses for the eliminations from Oct. 5-Jan. 7, also agreed the original course would be used for the finals beginning Jan. 31.

The other major difference between the Fremantle and Newport courses was the layout of the courses.

The Olympic-style Newport course had six legs, including the second and third crosswind or reaching legs. The first, fourth and sixth legs were windward legs, meaning they were sailed directly into the wind. The fifth leg was the only downwind leg, meaning it was sailed with the wind.

The Fremantle courses, including the alternates were designated to have eight legs, each slightly shorter than the Newport legs in order to maintain the modern 24.3-mile America's Cup course. The first, third, sixth and eighth legs were to be windward. The second and seventh legs were to be downwind. The fourth and fifth legs were to be the two reaches, which meet to form a triangular course; one reach was for taking the boats out and away from the straight legs, and the other reach was for bringing them back to the straight legs.

Designers had to rethink their race tactics because of the two extra legs. The yachts would have to make additional 180-degree turns and that called for improved turning capability. At the same time, the boats, masts and other equipment on board would have to be sturdier because of the added stress additional turns would place on them.

The sailors, too, were directly affected by the new course plan. They had to view their sailing responsibilities differently as well as their physical training. Not only would they be changing sails more often — the spinnakers are set on the downhill runs and reaches and taken down while working upwind — but the shorter legs meant less time to make those sail changes and to perform their other tasks. While the physical training for the sailors who participate in the America's Cup always had been extensive it was more so than ever for 1987.

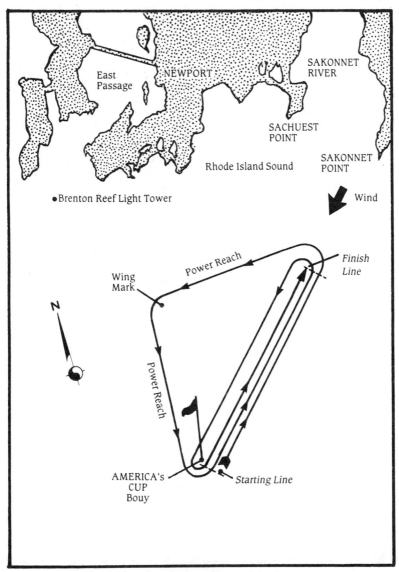

NEWPORT Race Course 1983 AMERICA's CUP

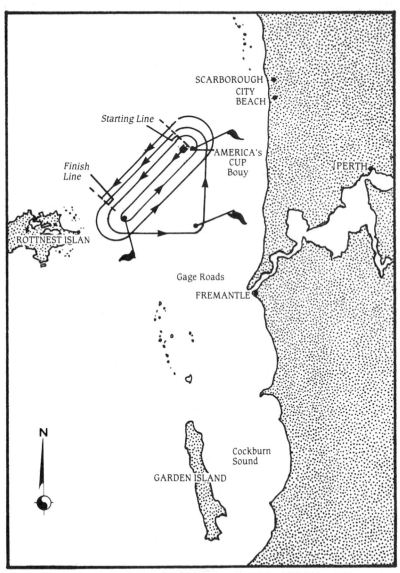

FREMANTLE Race Course 1987 AMERICA's CUP

Chapter VII

The Land Down Under

Australia is the charm of Fremantle, the friendliness of sparkling Perth, tropical rain forests in the north, kangaroos, beautiful Sydney on the east coast, wombats, the monotonous but fascinating red plateau of its interior, platypuses, aborigines, the Great Barrier Reef, sailing and the only continent where there has never been a war.

The America's Cup may have been locked up in a tall glass case in Perth, Western Australia, but there is no disputing that ownership was a national affair and cause for national conversation across this land marked by unending contrast. They have talked about it, written about it and loved to pull your leg about the Cup all over the land Down Under, which when viewed upside down looks a lot like the United States without Florida. That seems appropriate since, apart from the battle for the Cup, Aussies and Yanks get on as well as any two peoples on the planet. The Cup provided the window for the world to view this curious continent, which remains largely untouched by human device. The vast majority of the inhabitants have roots there dating back to less than 200 years, though Australia also is home to 230,000 aborigines (1984 estimate) whose ancestors walked the continent 30,000-40,000 years ago.

In 1983, when *Australia II* defeated *Liberty* much of this nation of 15.5 million people, but especially the state of Western Australia, viewed the coming of Cup as a national event of great proportions and an opportunity to show off the place. There is, by all accounts, a lot to show. Australia may be the smallest of the seven continents but in square miles it is the sixth largest nation in the world, about the size of the United States excluding Alaska.

America's Cup travelers therefore will have to be selective. Some in-country air distances from Perth and Fremantle are: 1,720 miles to Melbourne; 2,040 to Sydney; 2,185 to Canberra, the nation's capital; 2,575 to Brisbane; and 3,000 to Hobart, the capital of Tasmania.

There are six states in Australia, including Western Australia, Queensland, New South Wales, Victoria, South Australia and the island state of Tasmania, off the southeast coast. The nation's two territories are the Australian Capital Territory and the Northern Territory. The country also has a host of islands and a claim to the 2.4 million square-mile Australian Antartic Territory, which is mostly covered with ice.

The seasons of Australia are virtually the opposite of those in the Northern Hemisphere. Spring occurs September through November, summer from December through February, fall from March through May and Winter from June through August. Much of Australia is arid, receiving less than 20 inches of annual precipitation. The farther inland one travels, the warmer and drier it gets with summer temperatures reaching a scorching 118 degrees. In contrast, along some of the nation's 23,000 miles of coastline, particularly in the east, southeast and southwest, there occur what are considered to be among the most pleasant climates in the world. It's no wonder those areas are inhabited by the vast percentage of the nation's population.

Western Australia

Covering one-third of the continent, Western Australia is a land of magnificent contrasts from its Mediterraneanlike west coast to the rain forests of the southwest, from the oppressive desert of the interior, to the aboriginal lands and sprawling cattle ranches of the north, to the rugged northwest where kangaroos and other animals found only in this remote corner of the world are abundant.

In addition to offering the natural beauty it has always had, and the man-made beauty it has created in 200 years Western Australia, especially Fremantle and Perth, have been fixing the place up to ensure that travelers enjoy their visit during the America's Cup, perhaps enough to want to return some day.

The federal government of the Commonwealth of Australia and the government of Western Australia decided the state and nation could benefit greatly from the visibility the America's Cup would provide.

Western Australia assigned Minister D.K. Dans to be its minister responsible soley for Cup matters. Government and private tourism promoters invested tens of millions during the three years before the 1987 races selling Fremantle, Perth, Western Australia and Australia to the world. They felt that even if the Cup were lost — not many believed that would happen for some time — four months of world-wide exposure would reap untold economic benefits far into the future.

Toward that end, the federal government invested $30 million on community projects — new housing, roads, marina facilities, restaurant space, upgrading of existing infrastructure, communications capability, public safety measures, police services

183

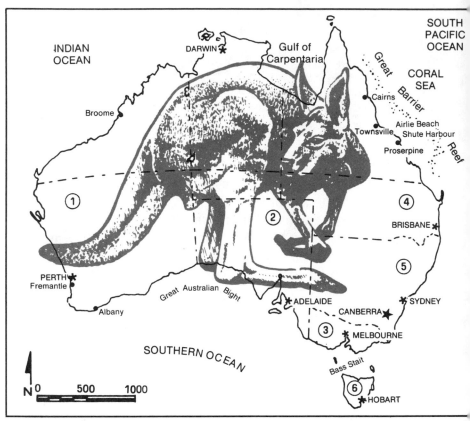

1. Western Australia   2. South Australia   3. Victoria
4. Queensland   5. New South Wales   6. Tasmania

and many other items. In order to cater to an international clientele, many of whom are accustomed to snapping their fingers for service, a government-assisted education program was undertaken to upgrade the skills of 2,500 people in the Perth and Fremantle hospitality industry. The state also involved itself in the redevelopment of hotels and other housing facilities, the accelerated completion and transformation of Perth Airport into an international facility, numerous impact studies and a long list of other assitance measures.

"Freo"

It was a race of sorts 158 years ago that led to the founding of Fremantle by the British and many hoped the many hoped another race would lead to its discovery by the world.

Both the French and British were familar with Western Australia in the early 19th century. Afterall, Dutch mariners had led the way as far back as the late 1600s. The British, leery of French interest in the area, decided to move quickly and claim the distant land for the crown.

Captain James Stirling, according to an official Fremantle historical account, "explored the coastal areas near the Swan River. His favourable report concerning the country surrounding the river was welcomed by the British Government, which had for some time been suspicious of French colonial intentions towards the western portion of Australia. As a result of Stirling's report, Captain Charles Howe Fremantle of *H.M.S. Challenger*, a 603-ton, 28-gun frigate, was instructed to sail to the west coast of New Holland (named by early Dutch mariners) to establish a settlement there." He did and was followed shortly by another visit from Stirling who then named the new settlement after Fremantle.

Fremantle, or Freo as the locals call it, is accustomed to change on the one hand and remaining the same on the other.

During its first 60 years there was little growth in the settlement of Fremantle. Unlike other parts of Australia where convict laborers were the first to populate many areas, the initial settlers in Western Australia were free people. Eventually, however, convict labor had to brought in to keep the west alive. Western Australia experienced little growth until late in the century. Gold seekers from around the world poured through the west coast in the 1880s and 1890s during the rush to Kalgoorlie and Coolgardie, about 325 miles northeast. Port facilities were constructed at Fremantle and by the turn of the century, the superb fishing in the area began to pay off. Moreover, the big steam liners began passing through regularly and the settlement at the mouth of the Swan River (a name stemming from the area's beautiful black swans) was transformed into the chief port of call for Western Australia. The decline in whaling and passenger liner traffic this century hurt, but Fremantle survived and today enjoys the status of being one of Western Australia's key fishing and shipbuilding centers. Despite that the city's economy was somewhat depressed in 1983.

Although the America's Cup has the potential of changing Fremantle forever in ways many do not desire, the city is accustomed to adapting to change while at the same time holding onto its past. That isn't just local booster talk: Fremantle won the prestigious Pacific Area Travel Association Heritage Award in 1983. It has managed to preserve its architectural and cultural heritage, and what the world would see when it focused in on the 1987 America's Cup is a rich blend of the past and present, including Victorian and colonial Georgian buildings persisting in the company of the structure and bustle of a modern maritime city.

The Fremantle Museum, built in the 1860s, is perhaps the best example of colonial Georgian architecture in an Australian setting. It has its own colorful history, having served as a lunatic asylum, a training hospital for midwives, a women's home and a base for U.S. naval personnel during World War II. Relics within the museum include the remains of 17th and 18th century Dutch wrecked ships.

Several blocks west is a marvelous example of 14th century Gothic architecture. St. Patrick's Catholic Church, built in 1902 to cater to the growing Catholic congregation in the colony, stands with dignity on Adelaide Street.

The oldest public building in the state is Fremantle's Round House, built in 1831 as a holding facility for lawbreakers, the structure actually is 12-sided.

Fremantle's preservation is owed largely to the City Council, which resisted the urban wave of the 1960s to bulldoze the past. Also, several buildings and landmarks neglected in recent years have undergone renovation in since 1983. Amid all of the planning and gearing up for the America's Cup, a group of preservation-minded citizens kept a watchful eye on local officials to guard against having Freo transformed beyond recognition when the boats were gone.

A bustling level of activity anytime, but more than ever since 1983, the city belies Fremantle's official population of around 25,000. Its proximity to the much larger city of Perth from which it draws a steady stream daily has a lot to do with that.

To go along with Fremantle's charming combination of past and present, the city is home to a mix of generations of Australians and immigrants, thousands of them, from Italy, Portugal, Yugoslavia, Southeast Asia, Greece and other countries.

The blend continues.

There's Fanny Samson's Rug Warehouse with straw on the floor, rugs draped over crates, barrels and wicker baskets, all intended to give the place the look of an eastern bazaar.

The Bannister Street Workshops is a turn-of-the-century brick, stone and iron building that houses a variety of craftspeople shaping pottery, turning wood, weaving, silversmithing and weaving wicker, and this in the presence of browsers or those who like to watch first-hand how what they buy is made.

The Fremantle Markets, open Fridays and Saturdays, date back to the late 1800s. Here there are paintings, gifts, antiques, food and a huge assortment of whatever's in season.

Stop at Papa Luigis, please. Otherwise you'll be greatly embarrassed someday when you meet up with another who has visited Freo, and who asks, "Wasn't Papa Luigis the best?" The delights here are primo; scallopine, pasta, veal parmigiana, calamari fritti, prosciutto and many delicioso desserts like espresso gelati. What makes it all taste so much better is the outdoor terrazzo where patrons dine.

Out on the waterfront you can enjoy fresh fish daily at Cicerello's Seafood Shanty amid incoming and outgoing fishing boats, sailing ships and other craft. Salvatore Cicerello and others left their homes in Sicily at the turn of the century and ended up fishing in the waters off Fremantle. The city's fishing industry is rapidly expanding, and already Fremantle is one of Australia's largest exporters of rock lobster.

While Fremantle's similarity to the Mediterranean is unmistakable — that's fitting since Freo's climate is much the same — the vast array of contrasting influences gives it a distinct cosmopolitan atmosphere as well.

Alongside all the activity surrounding the Cup, preparations were made for an event reminiscent of the first America's Cup race back in 1851.

Then it was the Great London Exhibition that brought a huge international contingent of businessmen, inventors and scientists to England.

Now the government of Western Australia proposed its brainchild, the Perth America's Cup International Exposition, which was expected to bring a similar group to Australia in November 1986.

Invitations were extended to nations challenging for the Cup, and Australia's trading partners and neighbors to participate in a massive showing of culture, industry, commerce, sport and entertainment all in an effort to promote new trading relationships. The invited nations were Bangladesh Brunei, Burma, Canada, France, West Germany , India, Indonesia, Ireland, Japan, Malaysia, Nepal, Netherlands, New Zealand, Pakistan, Papua-New Guinea, People's Republic of China, Philippines, Singapore, South Korea, Spain, Sri Lanka, Sweden, Taiwan Republic of China, Thailand, United Kingdom and the United States.

Workers in Fremantle Harbour built Victoria Quay Exhibition Centre, the venue for the exposition.

Meanwhile, the people of Freo, in addition to fixing the place up over for three years, fine tuned their welcoming and hosting skills when it became apparent a few out-of-towners could be expected. More like 500,000 from October to February, although some estimates put the total higher. Those skills and how the whole affair came off were apparently of considerable concern to the rest of the nation, which depends to a large extent on tourism and therefore hoped the western sector put on a good show.

Like any community Fremantle has its important and historic days, the date of founding, the year the first ocean lined docked among other. In 1983, everything else seemed to pale. Many citizens hoped 1987 would be recorded as the year the world fell in love with Freo.

Perth

It was to the silver of Perth, not the gold of Kalgoorlie, that 12-meter sailors and syndicate chiefs looked. what they coveted so much in a tall case at the Royal Perth Yacht Club on the Swan River. What they were seeking was being guarded there by an unwilling relinquisher in the club and 970,000 Perth people who are accutely aware of and proud of its presence.

While towns like Fremantle and others along the coast will be where the hordes stay by day for the Cup trials and finals, the vast majority will flock at night to Perth, the "City of Light," which turned all of its lights on in 1962 for astronaut John Glenn when he orbited the earth. He spotted them and told the world.

Perth is the capital of Western Australia. It is due northeast of Fremantle about 11 miles up the Swan River, which is more of an estuary than it is a river. Everywhere in Perth it seems there is water, and when you combine that with some of the world's most consistent "fine" weather, as they term it, you have daily, year-round bathers on white-sand beaches and sailboat hounds that crowd the Swan.

Perth, which has been compared to Dallas in appearance, is a clean, well planned and abundantly green city. Any criticism of the city lacking the sophistication of the world's big metropolises and of being a backwater town were likely to be dispelled following the America's Cup. Where it was lacking the city took great pains to improve.

Van Gogh, Picasso and Cezanne hang in the Western Australian Art Gallery and other cultural cneters. The city's other galleries, museums, playhouses and other facility give credence to the claim that you can enjoy the amenities in Perth and not feel rushed or crowded as you might in much larger cities.

The city's restaurants, some of the finest in Australia, boast an international cuisine. And if unenthused foreign yachtsmen and syndicate members weren't too fond of the service, as some indicated, Perth and Fremantle restauranteurs indicated they are a willing sort when it comes to pleasing visitors.

A pleasant way to spend an afternoon in Perth is walking, riding bikes or lazing on the grass on Mount Eliza at Kings Park. The park's 1,000 acres of lush bushland overlooks the city, the Swan River and the Indian Ocean.

Perth was founded two years after Fremantle and its growth follows a similar pattern. It was populated early by convict laborers, and later by the multitudes of gold rushers, some from Australia but many from around the world. While Fremantle remained relatively small, Perth grew quickly and that growth has continued to modern times. The city's 1972 population of approximately 500,000 has nearly doubled in less than two decades.

It is a remarkably clean city, which also has been likened to Los Angeles prior to smog. There are numerous skyscrapers but no billowing factories downtown. The industrial zone is 20 miles south of the city. The city itself is a financial center for most of the state's industries, including mining, ranching, agriculture and a fast-growing wine industry around Perth and elsewhere in Western Australia.

Like all of Australia, Perth is fairly psyched for tourists anytime, but it undertook extensive preparation also in order to be ready to receive as many visitors in four months as it typically gets in a year. Hotel and other overnight facilities were expected to at least double the number of rooms in the city to

10,000. Since the beginning of 1986 new restaurants seemed to be opening every other day.

The government of Western Australia wanted a better idea of how many visitors would descend upon Perth and Fremantle so it hired the Centre for Applied Business Research at the University of Western Australia.

The Centre arrived at the following findings:

"The expected number of Western Australia country visitors coming to Perth for the America's Cup is expected to lie within the range 113,000 to 125,000 with a mean estimate of 119,000. This is a 23 percent increase over the mean estimate of 512,000 such visitors who would be expected in Perth at that time if the Cup were not being held.

"The expected number of interstate visitors coming to Perth for the America's Cup is expected to lie within the range 329,000 to 397,000 with a mean estimate of 363,000, which is a three-fold increase over the mean estimate of 114,000 such visitors who would be expected in Perth at that time if the Cup were not being held.

"The expected number of international visitors coming to Perth for the America's Cup is 70,000, which is a 93 percent increase on the 76,000 such visitors who would be expected in Perth at that time if the Cup were not being held."

It all added up to a "mean," but certainly welcome, estimate of 552,000 visitors in Perth just for the America's Cup. That's a 78.6 percent increase above normal.

Australian officials didn't expressed any concern that overnight accomomdations would be inadequate for the event and that may be because the study found that 70 percent of the in-country visitors "intend to stay with friends and relatives with a smaller number (14 percent) expecting to stay in basic hotel/motel accommodations.''

Illustrating the high degree of interest the locals have had in the America's Cup, the Centre found, ''From responses on the past activity of Perth residents, it is clear that local interest in the America's Cup is very high; nearly three-quarters of the sample watched or heard the final race in 1983 (when Australia won the Cup). This interest is likely to be maintained during the Cup defence; 95 percent of the respondents expect to watch the Cup . . . Further, nearly two-thirds of respondents expect to visit the Cup facilities in Fremantle during the period.''

The study investigated a wide range of matters, including the perceptions people had of Perth. ''Respondents in general believe Perth is friendly, clean, has good restaurants, is relaxing and has a number of activities available both during the day and evening.''

Australian citizens also indicated they believed Perth would undergo some changes during the Cup activity. ''The most noticeable are related to the city becoming more expensive, more crowded, and more difficult to get around. However, they expect gains in terms of nightlife, the general level of excitement and the prevalence of a carnival atmosphere.''

After the Cup, the study found, 83 percent of the respondents expected Perth to be as good a place to live or better than it was prior to all of the activity and 40 percent believed it would be a better place.

Another interesting fact uncovered by the study was that ''Approximately 10 percent of Perth respondents stated they owned a boat.'' The Centre estimated that 28,000 private boats would be out on the water at some point during the event to watch challenge eliminations or the finals.

Rottnest

With all of the water in and around Fremantle and Perth vistors might wish for a ferry and their wish is granted, for there is year-round ferry service from both cities to magical Rottnest Island, one of the best-kept secrets in the world.

"Here it seems that nature has spared nothing to render this isle delightful above all other islands I did ever see . . . a terrestrial paradise," Dutch seafarer, Commodore Willem de Vlaming, wrote in his journal after landing on the island Dec. 29, 1696.

Vlaming named the small isle, Mist Island, but another notation in his journal led to its current name. He dismissed curious little animals he and his crew had seen as woodrats and upon reading this Dutch officials later renamed the island Rattnest, which eventually became Rottnest.

The little animals were neither rats, nor members of the rodent family, but quokkas or rock wallabies, which are marsupials and members of the kangaroo family. They were in danger years ago but now are a protected species and their number has grown to 9,000 on the island. The little critters, which appear mostly at night, have rough-soled feet enabling them to better negotiate the rock surfaces on the island.

Captain James Stirling spotted Rottnest 130 years after Vlaming but he was on business for King George IV and decided the island showed no prospect as a settlement. He paid it little attention.

Several years later a handful of settlers did go to the island where they farmed or collected salt. In 1840 Rottnest became a prison for Aborigines. It was officially closed in 1903. The island also has housed a boys reformatory, a World War I POW camp and it was the site of gun emplacements during World War II.

Soon after its use as a penal colony ended it was recommended that Rottnest be designated a tourist resort and steps were taken to protect its unique flora and fauna. It was declared an A-Class reserve in 1917, and while it has taken time for people to discover what Rottnest has to offer, the island's popularity has grown considerably in the past 25 years. The visitor total soared from 40,000 in 1960 to 400,000 in 1984.

Rottnest is approximately 6.8 miles long by 3.1 miles wide and lies about 11 miles off Fremantle. Visitors aren't permitted to drive motor vehicles there and very few will be found on the island. Getting around means walking, riding a bicycle or taking one of the few tour buses. Most people ride bicycles.

Rottnest is fairly small as islands go, about 4,765 acres, but it may be just the right size for the vacation paradise conceived around it. The best that nature has to offer has been combined with the best in pleasure and recreation.

There are more than 100 species of birds on Rottnest, including the red-capped robin, banded stilt, crested tern and cormorant.

Fauna on the island include the Rottnest Island tea and cypress trees, golden wattles, pink Boronias, yellow ragwort, native pigface, tufted spinifex grass and much more.

Among the several lakes on the island is Lake Baghdad on the north side. Its fresh water pools attract a good assortment of the island's wildlife, including fairy terns, the long-legged oyster wading bird, quokkas and many types of ducks among others.

A kilometer to the east is Garden Lake, which seems to be

a favorite of the many lovely swans on Rottnest.

Capt. Vlaming's fascination and adoration of Rottnest may have been solidified as he stood at what is now Vlaming Lookout, the island's high point, and surveyed the features of this strip of land sprawled out over the water to the west. Perhaps he sailed around to the island's west end and stood at Cathedral Rocks gazing westward out across the Indian Ocean during a tropical sunset when sun, sea and sky blend into a magnificent canvas of fiery and passionate hues. Did he wonder how far west he must sail before encountering land? It is more than a 5,000-mile journey due west to the east coast of South Africa at the bottom of the continent.

Among the many diversions on the island are swimming, fishing, boating, surfing, hiking, exploring, golfing, cricket, Australian-style bowling and tennis.

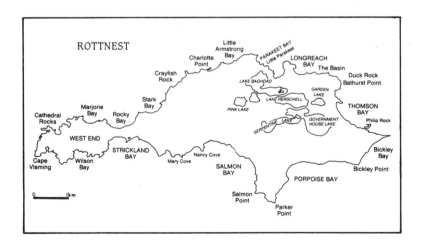

At very reasonable rates, a variety of overnight accommodations are available, including hotel and resort-style rooms, guest houses, cottages, cabins and campgrounds.

The Great Barrier Reef

Along 1,250 miles of Australia's east coast and stretching north to Papua-New Guinea is one of the great wonders of the world, the Great Barrier Reef, the largest concentration of coral islands in the world.

Here tiny invertebrate creatures of the sea known as polyps deposit coral to form long, spectacular stretches of coral cays that come in a wide variety of colors and shapes.

What strikes those who go "reefing" here for the first time is that the Great Barrier Reef seems to be alive, and indeed it is, teeming with life along great reaches of transparent, shallow water where a vast array of coral, huge sea clams, colorful fish, turtles, orchids and much more can be seen. Much of the plant, fish and marine life is unique to the area. Some of the plants seem more like animals as they withdraw instantly when touched. Close in or near the outer limit of the reef, which is anywhere from about 10 miles to 150 miles wide, you can peer through glass bottom boats, examine the sea life and formations from underwater observatories, pass over in low-flying scheduled flights or get an up-close look by scuba diving and witness a veritable marine extravaganza.

There are many towns, cities and ports all along the coast of the state of Queensland which visitors can use as bases from which to begin their Great Barrier Reef adventures. Cairns,

Townsville, Mackay, Rockhampton and Gladstone, all are comfortable and geared toward tourists, sportsmen or serious marine observers.

If an island is more to your liking, among the 18 that have been developed into resorts is Lizard Island. The rocky surface here was traversed by none other than the Captain James Cook, the explorer whose many sea voyages are so closely linked to early English settlement of Australia. Cook was said to have been in awe of this beautiful island, which is surrounded coral reefs, but he was also stranded inside the outer limit of the reef, off what is now the state of Queensland in northeast Australia. Cook climbed the highest point on the island in search of a passage out to the open sea.

Getting to most points along the reef is uncomplicated as ample air, train and bus service is scheduled all year.

Although there are sufficient accomodations to serve the growing stream of tourists, April through September is fairly booked so visitors planning to arrive those months should do so well in advance. Some resorts may close January through March.

Sydney

The birthplace of what was to become modern Australia was beautiful Sydney.

Australia was not unknown to the world in 1788 when the first convicts and free people arrived in Port Jackson and settled around nearby Sydney Cove. Chinese astronomers may have been on the continent long before the birth of Christ, and second century European geographers were known to have discussed and debated the existance of a faraway land called terra australis incognita (unknown southern land). Several European nations knew of or had sailed to or near Australia during the age of exploration, but only England chose to actively settle it, and the Sydney area was their choice for the first settlement.

The first years for the New South Wales colony were dark ones, and if it hadn't been for England's avowed policy of sending regular shiploads of convicts, and for the tenacity of the convicts themselves, survival of the colony was doubtful.

Its fair summers and mild winters, wooded peninsulas and peaceful coves were all too tempting to those who encountered them and Sydney quickly grew to become the continent's most populous and important city.

Sydney today is a bustling, economically healthy city, home to 3.5 million people, or more than 22 percent of Australia's population. It is a major international port, and the nation's manufacturing, business and industrial center.

The list of attractions in and around Sydney is lengthy, but at the top of it without question is the famed, legendary-in-its-own-time Sydney Opera House, a strong candidate to be grouped among the man-made wonders of the modern world. Completed in 1976, the Opera House soars with architectural grace and imagination 230 feet above Bennclong Point. The Opera House has six white sections of roof reaching out to the heavens, and giving the distinct appearance of a mighty, multi-sailed ship, appropriate enough since all of its perimeter, except the aft side, is surrounded by the waters of Sydney Cove and Port Jackson. Regarding its practical purposes, the Opera House has a 600-seat playhouse, 2,700-seat concert hall, 1,500-seat opera hall, restaurants, recital rooms and reception areas.

The heart of Sydney is compact enough that a walking trip would not be overly taxing, but one of the truly enjoyable ways to appreciate the city is to get out on the water, take one or more of the ferry trips, and there are many from which to choose, because commuting by ferryboat is a way of life for many residents here.

A popular section of Sydney where visitors can glimpse a rich, though not always upright, past is The Rocks. Here taverns, flophouses, hovels and brothels abounded in the middle of the 19th century, the streets were roamed by sailors, bands of thugs and outright rapacious blokes. At the turn of the century The Rocks was decimated by a scourge of bubonic plague and within a few decades many buildings had been leveled. Since the 1970s there has been some effort to revitalize and restore some of the old buildings of The Rocks and now antique shops, a variety of galleries, novelty shops and restaurants dot these previously untoward and scandalous streets.

Sit beneath a Moreton Bay fig tree at Observatory Park from where you can get a delightful view of the village greens, gas lamps and terrace houses down below at Argyle Place. From the Observatory, built in 1858, you can view beautiful Harbour Bridge, which spans one of the largest harbors in the world to link the city's two metropolitan sectors, North Sydney and Sydney.

See Parliament House, first occupied by the legisature in 1829, and witness the New South Wales state legislature in action. (No, Sydney is not the nation's capital. That's Canberra, 190 miles south. Australians take great pride in the fact that their national capital was planned on a budget of $3,500.)

Stroll through the Royal Botanical Gardens in mid-September when azaleas are in full bloom and see the more than 400 international varieties of plants, shrubs and trees in the 67-acre park.

Australia is famous for nothing if not for its unique wildlife, so there is little need to expound on the fabulous world of animals to be found in Sydney's Taronga Park Zoo.

The city's 34 golden beaches, filled with sunbathers in the warm season, would be a relaxing way to spend a weekend, but for an excursion away from the city, visit the waterfalls and expansive ravines of the Blue Mountains, which awaits visitors just 65 miles west of downtown Sydney. Head south 20 miles, and you can go bushwalking, camping or gaze at the gorgeous wildflowers in spring at Royal National Park. Just 15 miles north of Sydney is a colony of koalas, honeyeater birds, sandstone plateaus and wild bushland at Ku-ring-gai Chase National Park.

Tasmania

The land just down under the land Down Under is the state of Tasmania.

Due to its substantial rainfall each year much of Tasmania, which is about 200 miles south of the continent, is lush with vegetation.

Scattered around the island, which at its farthermost points is 184 miles long and 195 miles wide, are elms, oaks and poplars. Tasmania has the greenest valleys and hillsides to be found anywhere. There are rugged walls of mountains throughout the state and many of their snow-capped peaks rise in stark contrast to the tropical lowlands around them. Countless crisp, clear and clean streams are abundant with trout and attract fishermen from around the world.

Many of the 427,000 (1984 estimate) people living on the 26,178-square-mile island call themselves Tasmanians rather than Australians.

Whereas much of Australia, except the coast, is hot and dry, Tasmania is fair and moist. The eastern third of the state may receive less than 30 inches of annual rainfall, but much of the remainder receives 40 inches or more. While snow is rare over much of the continent, the snowfields of Tasmania can be more extensive than those of Switzerland.

Tasmania's capital city of Hobart in the south near the Tasman Sea was founded in 1804, and in addition to its modern high-rises many of its streets retain examples of its Georgian and Edwardian heritage.

One of the oldest remaining colonial homes in the city is Van Diemen's Land Folk Museum, a vintage 1836 residence containing artifacts depicting the lifestyle of the period's more affluent citizenry.

Visit Australia's first casino and Hobart's plushest hotel by stopping or staying at the 21-story Wrest Point Hotel-Casino.

One place most visitors to Tasmania pay a visit to is the old penal colony at Port Arthur, about 60 miles southeast of Hobart. Abandoned in 1877, the prison was one of the last in Australia. It was built by the prisoners, and in addition to the inmates' barracks it included a lunatic asylum, exile building, prison church and a secluded section where the so-called "silent system" replaced lashings. Ferocious dogs lined the only exit, a narrow land bridge, to discourage escapes.

Tasmania has been a vacation playground and holiday getaway for Australians for many years, and you can usually leave it to the locals to know where to go to have the best time.

Melbourne

"Seems to be quite English," many an Englishman or others familar enough to know must have said while strolling through stately Melbourne.

One might get that impression along the city's tidy streets with homes constructed after Victorian, Georgian and some Gothic revival tastes, or on a walk through Fitzroy Gardens where you find ivy imported from England and famous Cook's Cottage (after explorer Capt. James Cook) also brought from England and reassembled.

Yes, English tradition runs deep in this city of 3 million - free Englishmen traveled north from Tasmania and settled the original townsite 152 years ago -but Melbourne, capital of the state of Victoria, is as much Australian as wombats.

There are plenty of those bearlike marsupials as well as emus, kangaroos, fairy penguins, koalas and many other animals indigenous or imported at the Zoological Gardens, one of the finest zoos in the world.

If you've never heard the story of Phar Lap, Melbourne's great gelding, visit the National Museum on Russell Street. One of its biggest exhibits is on Phar Lap, who won 37 races in the 1930s and became a national symbol of greatness and courage. The museum also has a large and fine collection of distinctly Australian artifacts.

You can't get any more Australian than Australian Rules Football, and spectators of this game invented Down Under don't get any more passionate than they do in Melbourne where crowds often reach 100,000.

As big as football is and is getting in the city on the Yarra River and near Port Phillip Bay, "the" sporting event of the year is the Melbourne Cup, held the first Tuesday in November. Just as the America's Cup challenge trials would be heating up, and regardless of Australia's tremendous pride and interest in that Cup, the nation allows nothing to divert its collective attention from Flemington Racetrack for one of the top international horse races.

Another great attraction in Melbourne is the golfing. Water is to Syndey like golf courses are to Melbourne. Residents there contend that their city is the golf capital of the world.

America's Cup visitors who planned to be in Melbourne a few days were likely to see some real pros engaging in a bit of that most English of games, cricket. At beautiful Melbourne Cricket Ground where Australians play it quite well, cricket is in season from October through March. The Cricket Museum here will provide information on the game and some historical background.

Melbourne is loaded with enough parks and gardens, golf courses, municipal beaches, tennis courts, nearby fishing holes and other playgrounds to perk up any vacationer in a hurry.

Helping Melbourne to maintain its status as Australia's fashion center are a host of exclusive boutiques and a variety of other clothes stores for men and women on Collins and Bourke streets downtown.

Melbourne is quite active in the arts, particularly the theater, and some of the best in Australia can be found here. Companies from many nations perform in Melbourne's three major theaters, Her Majesty's Theatre, Princess Theatre and the Comedy Theatre. Just about anyone's tastes is catered to with a selection of symphony, ballet, dance, rock music and other brands of entertainment available throughout the year.

Darwin

You're in Darwin either during "the wet" or "the dry." There is virtually no in between in the capital city of Northern Territory.

Situated on the north central coast of Australia, tropical Darwin serves as a national and international point of takeoff for Southeast Asia.

During the Dry, April through October, Darwin is warm and pleasant, but in the Wet, November through March, monsoon season strikes and that means heavy rains.

Although it is a modern city, Darwin strikes many as still being more of an outpost, a place where you can get away from the world for a while.

Deep-sea fishing is excellent off the coast. The catch of most days includes, Spanish mackerel, coral trout and queenfish.

Less than an hour's drive southeast on the Stuart Highway is the Fogg Dam Bird Sanctuary where thousands of birds are found at the reservoir and buffalo roam the flat country.

Queensland

Much of the state of Queensland is a giant playground and one of its playgrounds of playgrounds is the Gold Coast, referred to by some as the Australian Riviera.

Gold Coast is a string of beach resorts at the southern-most point of the state's coastline. Needless to say, the subtropical climate here is very inviting — an estimated 5 million people visit the beaches of the Gold Coast each year.

Inland are the rain forests of the MacPherson Range where

you can watch beautiful Moran's Falls plunge into the gorge.

Fifty miles north of the Gold Coast is Queensland's capital, Brisbane, where slightly more than 1 million live. This pleasant and busy port at Moreton Bay is on both banks of the Brisbane River. A half-dozen bridges pass over the river, which has a steady stream of ferryboats, pleasure boats, freighters and liners.

In and around Brisbane there is a wide range of outdoor activities to watch or engage in, including lots of gardens to enjoy and parks, golfing facilities, race tracks, frequent rugby matches, swimming, tennis, cricket and sailing. The mild subtropical climate is quite accomodating, especially from April through November.

America's Cup Information Centre.
Fremantle, WA

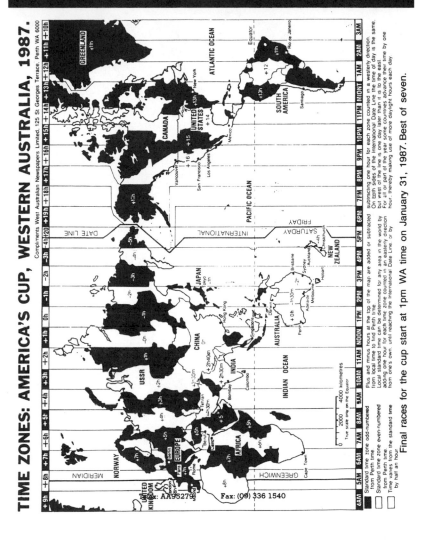

TIME ZONES: AMERICA'S CUP, WESTERN AUSTRALIA, 1987.

Final races for the cup start at 1pm WA time on January 31, 1987. Best of seven.